Special Education:
The Way Ahead

John Fish

Open University Press

Milton Keynes · Philadelphia

Open University Press,
12 Cofferidge Close, Stony Stratford, Milton Keynes MK11 1BY,
England
and
242 Cherry Street,
Philadelphia, PA 19106, U.S.A.

First published 1985

Reprinted 1987

British Library Cataloguing in Publication Data
Fish, John
    Special education: the way ahead. – (Children
    with special needs)
    1. Exceptional children – Education
    I. Title   II.   Open University   III.   Series
    371.9   LC3965

ISBN 0–335–15038–1
ISBN 0–335–15037–3 Pbk   319506

Library of Congress Cataloging in Publication No.
LC 85–5085

Text design by W.A.P.
Typeset in Great Britain at The Pitman Press, Bath

Printed in Great Britain by
Thomson Litho Ltd, East Kilbride, Scotland

DATE DUE FOR RETURN

09 FEB 95

11. OCT 95

08 FEB 96

This book may be recalled
before the above date

90014

Special Education:
The Way Ahead

Open University Press
Children With Special Needs Series

Editors

PHILLIP WILLIAMS
Emeritus Professor of Education,
University College of North Wales, Bangor.

PETER YOUNG
Formerly Tutor in the education of children with
learning difficulties, Cambridge Institute of Education;
educational writer, researcher and consultant.

This is a series of short and authoritative introductions for parents, teachers, professionals and anyone concerned with children with special needs. The series will cover the range of physical, sensory, mental, emotional and behavioural difficulties, and the changing needs from infancy to adult life in the family, at school and in society. The authors have been selected for their wide experience and close professional involvement in their particular fields. All have written penetrating and practical books readily accessible to non-specialists.

Contents

Series Editors' Introduction

The 1980s have seen revolutionary changes in special education, changes which have involved everyone concerned with the enterprise of educating children with special needs. But change requires effort. In making the effort required to implement new ideas and new procedures it is all too easy to concentrate our attention on the immediate task, whether that be introducing a new assessment procedure in our own education authority, developing a new curriculum for children with learning difficulties in our own school, or planning a co-teaching programme in our own classroom. A preoccupation with our own problems prevents us from seeing how others are tackling similar challenges: we have, therefore, less opportunity to share insights at a time when insight is most needed.

At such a time we need to be reminded that the challenges we face are not unique: others share our concerns and have developed their own responses, sometimes similar to ours, but sometimes different and sometimes more effective. This book describes the more important concerns that face special educators today and describes some of the more effective solutions that have been instituted. The solutions offered are not solely British; many of the examples are taken from the author's wide experience of developments in special education in different countries. Indeed, this is one of the strengths of the book. It continually reminds us, through a rich variety of international examples, that similar issues exist wherever children are educated, but that different groups of professionals think through the problems in a variety of ways. We can choose the examples and take ideas which apply to our own situation. The structure of training for special education, which has been instituted in Norway and which is outlined in chapter eight, is an example of a development which will interest many readers.

This book is more than a description of current practices, interesting though these are. The effort of reorganising our practices not only restricts our chance to learn what others are doing, it also limits the time we have for thinking about where we are going. It is easy, for example, to be so lost in the legal detail of making statements that the reason for introducing them is forgotten. We forget the wood and study the trees. So the author also looks at the changing purposes of special education, the way ahead. Few are better placed than John Fish to do this, for he occupies a position that is unique. As a former H.M. Staff Inspector for special education in England he has held high responsibilities: he was one of the Department of Education and Science's assessors on the Warnock Committee; at the time of writing he is the chairman of the Inner London Educational Authority's Committee reviewing provision in the metropolis for children with special needs; he is also heavily involved with the OECD special education project. These activities have given him the opportunity to reflect on a wide range of developments in the education of children with special needs, often seen at firsthand both here and abroad. As he himself says, the way ahead for special education is not clear. But from his unique perspective he sees more of the horizon than most, and sees it more clearly and in greater detail than most.

Several key pointers to the future emerge. Teaching arrangements will change as new practices enter classrooms. Training in special education will alter in order to introduce to the future the best of the present. Organisational structures in schools and areas will alter to take account of changing philosophy. It is this last phrase, a changing philosophy, which best catches the spirit of the book. It is the author's contention that the way ahead becomes clearer when we grasp the philosophy that *now* motivates the changing international scene. Just as the underlying principles governing changes in our local horizons become apparent with an aerial view, so the new conceptual framework that will determine the future of special education is clarified by the broad perspective adopted in this book. Seen in this way, the changes needed in pre-school provision, the greater involvement of parents – not least at the adolescent period – and the developments required in further education, all these and many other desiderata are seen to follow naturally from the basic philosophy.

This book enables us to see more clearly the underlying principles of special education and the changing practices that must follow from them. These changes concern us all, and the author's philosophy and the ideas that he outlines will enable us to grapple more effectively and more confidently with them.

Phillip Williams
Peter Young

CHAPTER 1

Setting the Scene

Special education is in a stage of transition in most developed countries. The United Kingdom is no exception. The Warnock Committee Report[1] and the 1981 Education Act are milestones and signposts reviewing progress and pointing the way to future developments. The next few years will see education and other services in England and Wales implementing the new legislation; it is vital that this process takes place in a climate of understanding and sensitivity. It is not enough to know the legislation and regulations and slavishly follow administrative procedures. It is also necessary to understand the major ideas and principles behind the procedural changes and to have positive attitudes and aspirations for the improvement of the quality of life and opportunities for those deemed to be handicapped.

This book sets out to review the major trends in thinking about disability and handicap, to look at the current range of provision to meet special educational needs and to suggest the major issues which need to be tackled as the education service moves into the twenty-first century. It poses more questions than it provides solutions. It does, however, provide an agenda for discussion by administrators, advisors, teachers, parents and other professionals concerned with disability. It is also relevant to others less directly concerned who create the political and social context for education in general and special education in particular.

Just as it is easy to become preoccupied with procedural matters and not give time to thinking about the ideas and aspirations which should inform them, so it is also easy to take a narrow national view of issues. The major ideas discussed particularly in chapter 2 are not unique to the United Kingdom; it is for this

1

reason that the second section of this chapter is devoted to international trends and developments. For the same reason illustrations of practices in other countries have been used. There are international trends in special education as in other fields. These will continue to influence our thinking about the place of those with disabilities in society. The more so as communications improve and international organisations improve their effectiveness as disseminators of ideas and practices. It is, therefore, important to be aware of international development when considering the way ahead for special education.

It is equally important to have a broad knowledge of special education in one's own country since it is easy to become preoccupied with practical problems within the limited radius of one's own sector, school or class. A very broad approach has been taken in the hope that busy practitioners will find it helpful to look at the wider context in which they operate.

The remainder of this chapter gives a brief review of international trends and developments in the recent past and discusses the major ideas behind the 1981 Education Act. The next chapter considers in more detail some of these ideas, such as the changing concept of handicap, the establishment of the rights of those considered handicapped, integration and participation. The discussion is then more sharply focused on the relationship between education and special education leading to two chapters dealing with needs and means of meeting them. This is followed by two chapters considering major issues in special education. The penultimate chapter examines the critical question of training personnel and the final chapter looks at the way ahead and attempts to identify an agenda for building on the 1981 Education Act and stimulating future developments.

International Trends and Developments

During the last three decades powerful trends and influences in most developed countries have led to an increased recognition of the rights of those who are handicapped. This recognition has resulted in steps to increase their participation in activities with others who are not handicapped, and to increase their access to education, employment, leisure activities and residential arrangements within their communities. Over the same period, research in the social sciences has identified the damaging effects of categorisation, labelling and segregation. Parents groups, voluntary organisations and disablement groups have campaigned for improved opportunities to participate in all aspects of society. These trends and influences have gathered increased strength because they are international and provide a new context for the objectives of special education.

Legislation has been enacted in many countries and some examples of new Education Acts may illustrate the recognition of the right of all children to education. In England and Wales the 1970 Education Act made local education authorities responsible for the education of all children however severely disabled. This Act not only recognised the right of every child to education but also required the local school system to provide it. In the same year a law in Italy also extended the scope of compulsory education. Although many states and school boards in the United States had pioneered earlier developments, it was not until 1975 that Public Law 94–142 guaranteed free public education to all children whatever their degree of disability. School Boards were made responsible for providing it and integration encouraged by stating that such education should be provided in the 'least restrictive environment'. During the same year new legislation in Norway removed distinctions between handicapped and ordinary pupils, abolished categories and gave parents of children assessed as handicapped the right to have their children educated in ordinary schools. Danish law which came into effect in 1980 transferred the responsibility for educating some disabled children from social welfare to education authorities, thus recognising the right of all to be educated within the education service. The 1981 Education Act is a further example of similar changes being effected in England and Wales.

This belief in the right of access to education, where possible in ordinary schools, is therefore common to a number of countries where legislation has followed changes in attitudes and better understanding of the needs of those with disabilities and significant difficulties. These trends also came together in the UNESCO Conference held in Spain in 1981 during the Year of the Disabled Person. A common declaration, known as the Sundberg Declaration, was drawn up. Among its articles, the first affirms the fundamental right of every person who is handicapped to education, training, cultural activities and information. Measures to implement rights should be aimed at reducing the handicapping effects of disabilities and maximising integration in society. In the planning of services those who are disabled should be consulted and involved in decision-making. There was no dissent from these principles which represent common aspirations at the beginning of the 1980s and reflect the changes that have taken place in the last three decades.

Major Ideas Given Expression by the 1981 Education Act

The Warnock Committee was at work from 1974 to 1978 in a climate of change and in an international context of new ideas and aspirations. The Committee's Report[1], widely accepted as well informed and constructive echoed many of these ideas in its recommendations and priorities. Although concentrating on special education in England, Scotland and Wales, it was in the mainstream of thinking about meeting the needs of those who are disabled. The 1981 Education Act does not cover all the Committee's concerns, only those which the Government was prepared to accept which required legislation. Nevertheless, it embodies powerful new ideas in its conventional legal terminology. It is important not to lose sight of these while developing new procedures.

The Act recognises a wider range of special educational needs, only some of which may be so severe and complex as to need the safeguard of special procedures for assessment and provision. The definition of special educational needs is not linked to specific causes and is relative to the needs of all children. The Act makes clear the responsibilities of ordinary schools to detect, assess and provide for special educational needs, it cautiously encourages the process of integration, and gives parents increased rights to share information and decision-making. It abolishes categories of handicap and broadens the range of special educational provision. Although for many, the Act does not go far enough in respect of integration and post-compulsory school age provision, and although it is largely taken up with procedural matters, it does by implication endorse broader themes. It is these themes which must be recognised and fostered if future developments are to display qualities of sensitivity, humanity and respect for the individual.

The first theme emphasises that there is only one population of children, *not* two populations or two kinds of children, the ordinary and the handicapped. Some members of this population may need special help because of disabilities or significant difficulties, but categories based on similar disabilities do not represent groups with the same needs. Thus the new framework endorses the right of all to education, while it stresses the pre-eminence of *common* needs. It sees disabilities and significant difficulties as variations in need and not as defining different kinds of children.

②Secondly, each child should be individually assessed so that, where special education is necessary, this can be planned to meet identified needs. There is no longer an assumption that a particular disability requires a particular curriculum or methodology. This reflects the World Health Organisation's differentiation between disability and handicap, a topic which will be discussed in more detail in the next chapter.

③Another major theme is integration. Previous legislation had assumed that separate provision in special schools was the first essential and that arrangements in ordinary schools were a secondary alternative. However, since that policy was stated in the 1944 Education Act it has been recognised that subsequent participation as an adult in the local community is not necessarily fostered by isolation during the school period. The issues surrounding the process of integration are complex. At this stage it is sufficient to recognise that the 1981 Act accepts recent changes in attitude, recent research and new social values. It suggests that one should look first to the ordinary school as a setting for special education and that a special case needs to be made for separate provision. Secondly, it recognises that the process of integration has to be fostered by planning shared activities. Placement in an ordinary school is no guarantee of positive interaction between those who are disabled and those who are not.

④Finally, the theme of participation is strongly endorsed. Parents and young people who are handicapped are to have more information and be more involved in making decisions. The education and treatment of those with disabilities is no longer an exclusive concern of different professionals. These notions of partnership, of expectations of competence and of respect for individual views represent major changes in attitude. Disability is no longer to imply incompetence in managing one's affairs.

Although these themes will be recognised by those closely concerned with special education, they are as yet not always understood by other administrators and professionals. Nor are they firmly rooted in the attitudes of the general population. The 'Does He Take Sugar?' syndrome is not uncommon. Preoccupation with the nuts and bolts of implementing the new Act should not blind us to the importance of keeping these themes in the public eye.

CHAPTER 2

Major Themes

Introduction

The recent history of provision for those categorized as handicapped and of changing attitudes to them reflects a struggle to gain a recognition of common human needs including participation in all facets of everyday life. Any society is uncomfortable with deviance and difference and tends to isolate individuals who do not conform to 'normal' expectations. But since the Second World War and particular in the 1960s and early 70s there were genuine moves towards a fairer society in which those with disabilities could share. These developments may now be less evident in a more competitive and less caring political climate. However, changed circumstances do not invalidate the legitimate desires of those who are deemed to be handicapped to share the same rights and responsibilities as other citizens. Their struggle has been made more difficult because society viewed and to some extent still views those it considers handicapped as objects of charity. Charitable foundations were the first providers of care and education, and charitable organisations continue to provide many facilities and resources for those with disabilities. The Christian virtue of charity has many positive characteristics and if more widespread would ensure a greater acceptance of those with disabilities in local communities. However, the institutionalisation of charity results in negative attitudes such as a preoccupation with maintaining prestigious facilities and an implication that those for whom they are providing should show a seemly sense of gratitude and dependence. Those who act as advocates, working with individuals who are disabled, have to battle with a sometimes stultifying bureaucracy to change an unthinking charity into a real concern for the freedom of the individual to choose and develop a personal life style.

In the following sections four major themes of this struggle are discussed. A recognition of individuality, of entitlement to normal patterns of daily living and of a right to work and participate in the communities in which handicapped people live are three of them. The fourth, and perhaps the most important, is a new and different concept of handicap. It is on this dynamic and more flexible concept of handicap that progress in the first three themes depends.

The Concept of Handicap

It is necessary to look briefly at traditional thinking from which recent changes have stemmed. A crude description of early beliefs might be that inherited characteristics and constitutional factors placed narrow limits on the expectations of those who were handicapped. The deaf could not talk, the cerebral palsied could not walk and the mentally handicapped could not think. Handicapped people were different from ordinary people, their limitations were God-given and they needed care and protection. Few of them were seen as able to participate in normal working and domestic life.

Many individuals in different professions sought to change these attitudes. The history of health care, social welfare and special education is full of examples of increased understanding and extended opportunities for learning and working. While resulting in much progress, the increasing involvement of professions has raised other barriers to a common understanding of the concept of handicap. Professional groups established exclusive areas of influence and tended to become guardians and gate-keepers to life for their clients. Teachers, for example, decided on theoretical grounds whether oral or manual methods were appropriate for the hearing impaired. It was the professional groups who tended to segregate disability into categories assuming that children and young people with similar disabilities had identical needs and that their future pattern of living should be wholly determined by specialist skills and opinions. This is a relatively crude summary, and gives little weight to the range of views and aspirations of many pioneers, but it does reflect the important point that the increasing involvement of skilled professionals in the field of disability did not at first increase the opportunities for individual choice and participation.

Major developments in sociology and psychology in the 1950s and '60s pointed out the adverse effects of categorisation, labelling and institutionalisation. The effects of disabilities could be made worse by low expectations, by inappropriate social attitudes and by unsuitable forms of provision. These developments were accompanied by the formation of pressure groups of parents and disabled individuals themselves campaigning for greater access to education, employment and other opportunities. All these influences led to a greater recognition of individual differences, of the potential of those with disabilities and of the handicapping effects of social circumstances.

This brief analysis is an introduction to the important distinction between disability and handicap which was formalised by the World Health Organisation in the 1970s. *Disability* was defined as a loss of function or activity by the individual as a result of impairment. Such losses of function or activity were seen as not only resulting from obvious impairments of sight, hearing or physical functioning but also from intellectual impairments, such as mental retardation and learning disabilities, and emotional and motivational impairments, such as mental illness and disturbed behaviour. The term *handicap* was defined in terms of the effects of personality characteristics and social situations on a disabled individual. Thus individual differences in intellect, temperament and character, family circumstances, socio-economic status, forms of intervention and provision, and administrative procedures, may all determine the extent to which a disability is handicapping for an individual.

The distinction between disability and handicap is crucial to the understanding of individual special educational needs and to the development of arrangements to meet them. Although in many ways the distinction is no more clear cut than that between nature and nurture, in that it involves a dynamic interaction between the individual and his environment, it has important consequences. It recognises that the handicapping effects of a disability may change over time from childhood to adulthood and as a result of different forms of intervention. Finally, it includes the idea that handicapping effects may vary from situation to situation. Thus the different effects in education, employment, living and leisure circumstances can be understood, while the importance of elements in those situations which are handicapping and amenable to change can be identified.

Because the handicapping effects of different circumstances on the individual with a disability vary it may be helpful to list some of them under the following headings:

1. *Individual differences*

Without entering into the nature–nurture issue, it is reasonably certain that individual variations in intellectual performance, in temperament, in personality and in strengths of drives will be evident as children grow up. Although these differences are themselves attributable to an interaction between inherent potentials and experiences, the resulting pattern of an individual's abilities, characteristics and attitudes will have a marked influence on the degree to which his disability is handicapping.

2. *Family differences*

Patterns of child rearing vary as do parent–child relationships. There will be at least two ways in which a particular pattern of family life may influence the degree to which a disability is handicapping. The first concerns the effect it may have on the intellectual, emotional and social growth of all children in the family and the second relates to the response of the family to the presence of a child with a disability. Each may affect the degree to which a child is handicapped.

3. *Social differences*

Although linked with family differences, there will be the influence of the extended family, friends and neighbours. Their attitudes and expectations and their interaction with the child with a disability also affect the extent to which the condition is handicapping.

4. *Intervention variables*

Early counselling and support for families, intervention programmes and supporting services of all kinds from birth to adult life will all be significant. The more effective the inputs, the less the handicapping effects.

5. *Administrative variables*

However successful the family and professional services, administrative procedures and criteria may have handicapping effects.

Legislation and regulations which imply standards of performance and behaviour may create barriers in addition to obvious
factors such as access to building and transport. Institutions, for
, example schools, may through their programmes and normative
criteria turn disabilities into handicaps.

This list is not exhaustive, but these five groups of factors do
illustrate the complexity of the changed concept of handicap and
underline the contributions of families, communities and patterns
of social organisation to the degree to which an individual with a
disability may or may not be handicapped.

Perhaps all these complex relationships between disability and
handicap can be best illustrated by the leaving programme in two
special schools in different states of Australia. Both provide for
mild and moderate degrees of intellectual disability and have
programmes for the 16–19 age range. Both, at the time of a visit in
1983, were working against a background of increasing youth
unemployment. Both were making serious attempts to prepare
for transition to adult and working life.

The first school had a programme of work experience based in
the school with each class group undertaking general and social
education together with contract work in packing, printing and
woodwork among other activities. However, the disabilities of
the school population were seen as very limiting, and success was
measured by placement in sheltered workshops. Possibilities for
open employment were not studied or tackled. Although much
was being done, disability and handicap were being equated.

The second school had a two-stage course, the first of which
involved simulated work experience in school. The second involved paid work experience placements for up to three days a
week in local shops and factories, linked with social training and a
programme to develop independent living skills. As a result
about a third of all leavers entered open employment. Open
employment was analysed, the skills necessary developed, and
the barriers overcome at least for some young people. The
handicapping effects of disabilities were modified in a variety of
ways.

The belief in the distinction between disability and handicap in
the second case had a marked effect on the nature of the school
programme, its relationship with the community in which it
worked, its contact with parents, its aspirations and its results.
This distinction is therefore neither theoretical nor academic but
one which, once recognised, may have a profound effect on
educational aims, methods and arrangements.

It may be helpful to summarise this section with three axiomatic statements which result from distinguishing handicaps from the disabilities from which they may arise:

1. The handicapping effects of disabilities will vary with the nature and degree of disabilities. The more severe the disabilities the more adverse may be the effect of handicapping variables and the more important will be appropriate interventions.

2. Handicapping effects change over time and will not be the same at all ages. They may become more or less severe at different stages of development, for example, adolescence may be a time of considerable stress for someone with severe physical disabilities. The search for adult identity may result in new perceptions of long-term problems on the part of the individual and an increasing sense of being handicapped. But equally, handicapping effects may be increased by adult and social attitudes which restrict opportunities for personal fulfilment because of preconceptions which restrict opportunities for personal fulfilment because of preconceptions about limitations.

3. Handicapping effects change with varying situations. A disability which results in marked learning difficulties in school may not interfere with recreation or employment. A disability may be more handicapping in obtaining work than in living independently and vice versa.

Thus a dynamic concept of handicap which is changing, individually determined and situation specific is crucial if we wish to minimise the effects of disabilities through education, training and environmental change.

The Re-establishment of Human Rights

Before turning to the discussion of the rights to education, training, independent living and participation it may be helpful to note briefly another right which is a current concern, namely the right to be born. In the early days of provision for those with disabilities this issue never arose. Now, however, ante-natal investigations, amniocentesis and the possibility of terminating pregnancies have introduced a new set of practical, emotional and ethical issues. Advances in health care have both ensured the survival of more profoundly and multiply handicapped children and, in some cultural and social circumstances, have offered a choice as to whether such children should be born. This is not the context to discuss the complex issues involved. It is perhaps helpful to recognise at the beginning of a discussion of rights that the right to be born disabled is no longer unquestioned.

The Right to Education

Although the provision of a form of education or training has long been a feature of arrangements for children with disabilities, the right to education has taken longer to establish. In many countries, including many developed countries, this right is not yet established for all children. In practice there are three aspects of this right which need separate consideration: the age range over which it operates; the degree of disability to which it applies; and whether it is included in mainstream educational legislation.

Although the position in England and Wales is now much clearer, it is worth recalling that the 1944 Education Act included the idea that children with severe degrees of mental retardation could not be educated. The right of all children, however severely disabled, to education was only established by law in 1970. A similar right was established in the USA by Public Law 94–142 in 1975. In both cases the entitlement to free public education brought all children with disabilities and learning difficulties into the mainstream of educational legislation. Both the 1970 and 1981 Education Acts included special educational provisions and made local education authorities in England and Wales responsible for such provision as part of a range of educational services. Only the age range over which these responsibilities should be exercised remains a major issue.

Although a number of other countries including Denmark and Norway have made education freely available to all within the main educational system regardless of the degree of disability, there are still many countries with highly developed educational services where children assessed as severely handicapped by medical and psychological services are excluded from the education system. In many cases education and training is provided by health and social welfare services but the unequivocal right to education does not exist for all children with disabilities.

According this right to all children challenges traditional views of education and stretches the concepts of learning and teaching far beyond the basic skills of literacy and numeracy. It redefines education as any systematic intervention provided to enhance personal growth and development. Most important, however, from the point of view of parents, is that appropriate programmes for their children provided by the education system within schools represents a normalisation process. It indicates an acceptance of individual differences and a recognition of the right to be educated.

In England and Wales the outstanding issue is the extension of this right beyond the compulsory school period of five to sixteen years of age. The importance of early intervention programmes is now widely recognised and the 1981 Education Act endorses the importance of pre-school provision for children under five years old. The Act empowers local education authorities to assess and provide educational services for children below the age of two if the parents wish for them. Similarly, because parents do not have to ensure that their children receive education before the age of five, local education authorities only have to provide special education if the parents wish it and they have assessed a need for it. Although the Act gives parents the right to ask for assessments of special education needs, which cannot be refused if reasonable, provision below the compulsory period continues to depend on parental wishes. Local education authorities may or may not be active in ensuring that parents of children with disabilities are made aware of the importance of early intervention. In times of limited resources provision may also be uncertain and patchy. Thus, the right to early intervention is not clearly established although its importance is recognised by the legislation and the conditions for its provision are established.

At the post-compulsory school stage, a right to education up to the age of nineteen exists. Parents can request it for their children but the local education authority decides whether this is provided in schools or colleges of further education. Again much depends on the keenness of parents. The local education authority's powers to provide special education for this age range require stimulation by consumer demand. Although many authorities are active in establishing post-school provision, young people with less interested and less effective parents may not receive continued education over this period.

The last thirty years have seen marked progress in establishing the right to education for those categorised as handicapped in many countries and there has been an increase in the age range over which services are provided. In one or two countries this right clearly exists between the ages of two and twenty-one. In others it now exists for the compulsory school period. Yet in a number of countries criteria for educability still exist and children with severe and profound disabilities are excluded from the education system. The position in England and Wales has been constantly improving since the 1970 Act and much will now depend on how active parents become in stretching the system above and below the compulsory age range.

The Right to Work

Paid employment remains both a legitimate expectation for most young people completing education and training and a significant sign of achieving useful adult status in the community. Currently, new technologies, less labour intensive industries, businesses and services, and changing patterns of trade and industry are causing a reappraisal of the goal of full employment. It is not proposed to discuss this major issue here, which is of great relevance to young people who are disabled, but it is necessary to establish the idea that they should have a fair share of all the opportunities available to their contemporaries. Perhaps there never has been and never will be a right to paid employment but, while social usefulness continues to be gauged by the ability to earn sufficient to lead an independent life, it will continue to be a legitimate aspiration of those who are disabled. It is the establishment of this legitimacy which has been a major trend in recent decades.

It has taken a long time to break out from a pattern of sheltered workshop provision where the disabled with low pay and dependent status often had few opportunities to use their potential. Progress was first evident with young people with visual and hearing disabilities who achieved academic success and some access to the professions. This was followed by young people with physical disabilities and the range extended to include technical and vocational education leading to open employment. More recently the idea of training for open employment has extended along the range of intellectual disabilities to include many of those with severe degrees of impairment. All this progress has been due to improved education and training programmes but it should not have been achieved if expectations had not been raised and the handicapping effects of different situations recognised and tackled.

Although the right to work may not exist, the right to be given equal opportunities to obtain work is being established in a number of countries through anti-discrimination legislation. For example, in the United States of America legislation makes it illegal to exclude from consideration for employment any suitably qualified applicant who is disabled, and steps to introduce similar legislation in Britain are being considered. This legislation would parallel Acts concerned with discrimination against ethnic minorities and women. Equal opportunities need to be established.

Whatever employment conditions exist, there remains a need to change attitudes and expectations and to seek openings in new fields of employment where those with disabilities may find jobs. New technologies will help but only if there is a willingness to accept the right of young people with disabilities to seek a wide range of employment opportunities.

One of the major drawbacks has been thinking in terms of categories seen as homogeneous. 'The deaf can't', 'the blind can't' and 'the mentally handicapped can't' are examples of sentence beginnings which are becoming much less common but, nevertheless, remain in widespread use by the general public. In all cases individuals have proved expectations wrong and perhaps now there is a greater tendency to identify positive characteristics.

Some brief examples may be helpful. In Japan one of the most common training courses for the blind is acupuncture. The sense of touch is considered more sensitive in establishing points to apply needles than vision. How far in other countries is that potential to develop a particular high level skill recognised? In a regular high school in the mid-west of the USA a course for the intellectually disabled (in UK terms the least able in former schools for the moderately educational subnormal and the most able in schools for the severely educationally subnormal) uses training sites outside school to develop mobility, and social and vocational skills. One such site at the time of a visit was a hotel bedroom which the group of students were trained to service. The training programme was systematic and thorough. What happened at the end of the course? Not everyone obtained employment but some students did. On the author's return to his hotel he found that his room and three others were being serviced daily by a young woman with Downs Syndrome, last measured IQ 30+, who travelled independently to and from work and met the exacting standards of a house-keeper who was highly satisfied with a conscientious and regular worker.

These examples illustrate raised expectations for employment, the use of effective education and training techniques and changed attitudes to work potential. They illustrate major changes which are taking place in many centres in different countries. But for the majority of young people considered handicapped, opportunities are more restricted, training more narrowly conceived and expectations more pedestrian. The potential of those with disabilities and significant difficulties to be successfully employed should be recognised and their skills developed by effective training schemes. The right to be prepared for work needs to be more widely accepted and a fair share of youth employment opportunities made available.

The Right to a Normal Pattern of Living

In many developed countries it is becoming increasingly difficult to define a single normal pattern of living. Although the basic family unit remains the most common form and a common aspiration, a significant and increasing number of children are reared in second marriages or by single parents. These changes during childhood obviously influence growth and development particularly for those with disabilities. Important as these social changes may be, they are less important than the significant moves over the past two decades to ensure that children and adults who are deemed to be handicapped live in the community with a normal pattern and rhythm of daily activities.

In the previous century, when alternatives to family care with no special services were first developed in a systematic way, the solution was the residential institution, hospital, boarding school or social welfare home providing total alternative special care. This separate and isolated provision established patterns of education, training and care which were positive and enlightened in their times. The best life-style to be offered was an alternative and sheltered one, with training for a limited range of occupations in special workshops and centres the main objective. A life-time of dependence was envisaged.

Although day-time special education and training developed, a single alternative continued to exist for the young adult until comparatively recently. The individual either lived at home, cared for by parents and relatives, or lived in a residential institution when such care was no longer possible or available. The same psychological and social pressures which questioned the concept of handicap in the second half of this century also stressed the limiting effects of residential institutions. Evidence emerged on the effects of institutionalisation and the concept of 'normalisation' was born.

Again it is not proposed to discuss the extensive literature which gave rise to the major changes now taking place in many countries. The results, however, are very significant for special education. Fewer young people are now entering large residential institutions. Many different arrangements are now being made for small groups to live in houses and flats in the community and for individuals to live independently. Supporting services are being developed to train and help young adults who are disabled to live as normally as possible in ordinary or adapted community housing. The right to a normal pattern of living is inherent in the social welfare policies of many services. In practice this normalisation principle can be applied from an early age. In Sweden, for example, services for those who are mentally handicapped often purchase houses or flats in the community. Small groups of children live in them with residential care workers, going to school daily and taking an increasing part in family life as they get older. To see these groups at home helping with domestic tasks and to see their care workers meeting them at school and talking with their teachers is to have a clear vision of a normal, non-institutionalised pattern of living, which eventually leads to a natural pattern of adult life.

In New Zealand the Society for the Mentally Handicapped has a similar approach with young adults. One example is the purchase of a small motel in a city suburb where pairs of young adults share each unit, caring for themselves, going out daily to workshops and joining community recreation facilities. A married couple also live on the site and provide continued training in domestic skills, supervise individual catering and teach independent living skills.

The concept of readiness for this degree of independence is challenged in Queensland, Australia, where the mental handicap service does not wait for the effects of training in hospitals. It takes groups of six or seven young adults out into leased houses, and provides twenty-four-hour staffing and training, reducing staffing and supervision as individuals become more competent. A normal rhythm of life is thus established at the outset. Seeing these groups in their own home gossiping over a cup of tea, albeit some with sign language, after their return from day centres illustrates the qualitative importance of normalisation.

Of course similar examples can be found in the United Kingdom but there still remains a tension between such arrangements and separate communities and villages such as those set up by Rudolf Steiner groups and the Home Farm Trust. These also establish more normal patterns of daily life with shared work and life with other adults. However, they exemplify enlightened separate provision rather than community participation. The right to a normal pattern of living is now recognised, although not always clearly established as an objective of services for those who are handicapped. Nevertheless, it is currently a major theme with profound implications for the education and training of those who are disabled.

Participation

The major trends away from separate and isolated provision for those deemed handicapped towards special arrangements within services common to all has been encapsulated in the concept of integration which became a major focus for discussion in the 1950s, '60s and '70s. Much has been written on this topic particularly with respect to education. Two books, in particular, summarise the major issues: Hegarty, Pocklington and Lucas in *Educating Pupils with Special Educational Needs in the Ordinary School* present a review of arrangements in England and Wales[2]; while *The Education of the Handicapped Adolescent – Integration in the School*[3] assesses international trends and innovations. It is not proposed to restate the arguments for moving towards integration in schools and other social institutions. They will be touched on in later sections where they are relevant to the development of special education.

However, it is necessary to recognise that fostering the process of integration is a natural consequence of the situational and relative concept of handicap already discussed. To place individuals into separate special schools and institutions is to isolate them from natural interactions with their contemporaries unless active and imaginative steps are taken to overcome social isolation. Effective teaching and care programmes are no longer enough. Without natural day to day interaction with their contemporaries many of those with disabilities may get false notions of the real world and prejudice and myths may be built up by those ignorant of them as individuals. There is a clear imperative to promote the process of societal integration in the long term. To do this requires that the handicapping effects of disabilities should not be unnecessarily increased by separate provision unless no other course is practical.

Within the education system the same social trends which accorded more rights to the disabled also led to greater emphasis on social values generally. Thus, the development of comprehensive schools was an integrative process. Although there is evidence of a swing back to 'basics', educators still retain a strong belief in the social values of schools. Among these values the understanding and acceptance of individual differences and the importance of individuals regardless of their achievements are significant. Thus, the truly comprehensive school provides for a wide range of individual abilities and conditions including disabilities.

Understanding the issues inherent in the process of integration is necessary in all schools regardless of the degree of disability or difficulty with which they may be prepared to cope. The right to free public education for all, expressed in legislation, demands that the system develops a policy for those whose disabilities may result in educational handicaps. Even where short-term considerations result in separate provision, the long-term objective of participation in society should not be lost sight of since few would now advocate separate provision for life.

Much thought and energy has been devoted to discussing integration both in terms of the nature and degree of disabilities, when and how it should take place, and what it might cost. There are many practical issues to be resolved but in principle the issue is simple. If those who are disabled are to be accorded dignity as individuals and to be given the same rights to education, work and the quality of adult life as others, then this can only come from increased participation in normal everyday life. To increase this participation is the objective of the process of integration. The process must be begun within the ordinary school.

What Sort of Life?

The last major theme of great significance to special education is the kind of life for which those who are handicapped are being prepared by the programmes and services available from soon after birth to early adulthood. It is often said that schools are slow to change, and slow to respond to altered circumstances in adult and working life. Many still prepare young people for a society which may not exist when they leave the education service. It is, therefore, increasingly important to keep abreast of major social changes and to choose as objectives for education in general, and special education in particular, those which prepare young people to cope with the world they will enter.

The major trends in the last decades of the twentieth century which will influence the kind of life possible for young adults with disabilities are now relatively clear. Employment for all is less certain because of economic conditions, changes in the labour market and the increasing use of new technologies to replace workers. At the same time new technologies are likely to increase the abilities of many who are disabled to manage their environment and to develop greater independence and interaction with others. Research continues to demonstrate that it is not the acquisition of skills necessary to specific jobs which limit employment possibilities. It is inadequate social and life skills.

In developed countries this leads to certain conclusions, in the light of the major trends already discussed in this chapter. We need to develop opportunities to lead a worthwhile life with or without paid employment. While always seeking to achieve an equitable share of available employment for those who are handicapped, acceptable alternatives need to be sought; alternatives which are similar to those for all young adults in local communities which are not segregative. One example is the development of independent and small group living arrangements, meeting the right to a normal pattern of life. For many who are severely disabled this will constitute a major daily effort. It will be useful work. For others it will accompany open or sheltered employment. Thus, one practical answer to the question 'What sort of life?' is a life of increased independence from families and less dependence on large residential institutions. This leads to the need for a curriculum, both in special education and post-educational training, which is focused on social and life skills, and to the need for financial arrangements and services channelled to support individual and small group living rather than institutions offering care. This is an area of work which can improve in effectiveness regardless of the employment situation and which can give point and purpose to special education.

Obviously the issues raised here need more detailed discussion. In an international context an OECD/CERI project on 'Transition to Adult and Working Life' will, by late 1985, have produced literature on the way these issues are being dealt with and giving examples of significant innovations. All that is attempted here is to register *transition* as a major theme which, together with the others already discussed, provides a context for special education. Special education, too often narrowly confined to the effects of specific disabilities and to the nature of special interventions within the education system, must look more broadly at the future life of the young people it serves. The development of its services and programmes needs to take more account of life after education. The current emphasis on further education is an important first step but more emphasis is needed on the preparation for living in a changing world.

CHAPTER 3

Education and Special Education

The relationship between education and special education has undergone major changes since the latter was first included in major educational legislation in 1944. It remains difficult for many to define special education partly because of traditional views on handicap and partly because of uncertainty as to how education for all children should be defined. Because provision for those considered handicapped is now no longer so separate, and because more arrangements for them are being made in ordinary schools, it is necessary to re-examine the relationship between education and special education.

Education

The long infancy and dependence of the human being results in learning being a central feature of the acquisition of knowledge and skills for adult life. All behaviour is learned to a greater or lesser extent. Because there is so much to be learned and because, for most, simple exposure to stimulation does not necessarily result in learning, a selection of what might be learned and some arrangement of learning experiences is necessary. It is the selection of experiences and the mediation of adults in helping to interpret them which is central to education, a process begun more or less systematically by parents, formalised in school systems and continued to some extent in adult life through interaction with others.

There is and will continue to be discussion about the selection of experiences, systematised in subject areas and curricula. This discussion involves questions of balance between the acquisition of knowledge and the development of study skills and between academic subjects and personal, social, vocational and life skills. However, the essential features of education remain the careful selection of learning objectives, the planning of learning experiences and the effective mediation of teachers. These features represent common ground shared by education and special education.

Education and Training

A distinction between education and training is seen by some as important and by others as of doubtful value. It is important to examine the two words since the history of special education includes a time when it was thought that not all children could be educated. Those who could not be educated could be trained. More recently some forms of behaviour modification have again raised the question of whether education and training should be seen as synonymous.

There seem to be two good reasons why they should not be equated. The first, and most significant, relates to the degree of freedom accorded to the learner to be active and to choose personal solutions to problems for himself. One common concept of training involves the development of a single response or pattern of activities in specified situations to produce habits of behaviour. Although this may be an element in education, most of us would expect it also to encourage personal interpretation, choice and judgement.

The second reason concerns the relationship between the teacher and the learner with particular reference to dependence. Training often implies a subservient relationship as anyone who has undergone basic training in the services will recognise. This is of special significance in work with children and young people who are handicapped. They are often dependent on adults as a result of disabilities and any programme which increases this unnecessarily is undesirable. First, then, it is necessary to distinguish clearly between behaviours which need to be habituated (trained) and those which do not. One can be trained to acquire social skills but not necessarily educated in their appropriate use. In this context we may regard it as ironic that we commonly refer to teacher *training* (as in chapter 8 of this book).

Special Education

Many people have confused ideas about special education. This is partly due to its history, partly due to changing professional responsibilities for children with disabilities, and partly because of recent changes in its relationship to ordinary education. The first two reasons are closely related since the care and education of those designated by society as handicapped has involved a major change from medical supervision to education responsibility. The third reason also has an historical perspective since the change from segregated separate provision, not always the responsibility of public education services, to provision as part of local education authority services has changed the relationship between special and ordinary education.

A comprehensive and succinct review of the history of special education can be found in Chapter 2 of the Warnock Report. It is not proposed to cover the same ground here. However, one or two comments are necessary to account for current misconceptions. First, although the 1944 Education Act made local education authorities responsible for discovering and providing for children who required special educational treatment, the decision to recommend such treatment and to categorize children usually remained a medical one in practice. A medical examination could be all that was required to determine whether a child was handicapped. This diagnostic responsibility naturally gave rise to a strong medical influence on the nature of treatment to be provided and to the use of the term 'special educational treatment' which remained a legal term until the 1981 Education Act was passed. In the interim between the two Acts, the 1970 Education of Handicapped Children Act removed the final medical responsibility for training handicapped children deemed to be ineducable. Thus, although special schools have a long history, and teachers in them have been increasing their knowledge and skills for many years, the responsibility for deciding which children required special educational treatment remained a medical one until very recently. Since 1944, local education authorities and teachers have been taking more and more responsibility for determining special educational needs, but it was only in 1981 that the law made these assessment responsibilities unequivocal.

During this period other developments took place which also confused the situation. There has been a big increase in the number of professions which have made and continue to make a significant contribution to programmes for children with disabilities and difficulties. Among these are educational and clinical psychologists, speech, physio- and occupational therapists, social workers and nurses. Many of these professions also moved from medical auxiliary status to separate professional identities and many have also had managerial responsibilities for special schools and programmes. As a result, the relationship of educational activities to therapeutic activities has often been confused. Some of the relationships continue to pose problems, for example, the relative contributions of physiotherapy and physical education to programmes for children with physical disabilities, of speech therapy and language teaching to programmes for children with language disabilities, and therapy and education in programmes for those with emotional and behaviour difficulties. However, the position is now more clearly defined. Although these professions will have important contributions to make to assessment and programme planning and responsibilities for elements in a child's total programme, the central focus of special education is educational. Children deemed to have special educational needs are entitled to and require an educational programme as similar to that of all other children as is practicable. Special education is now being defined in curriculum terms and teachers are seen as having the principal responsibility for curriculum development.

Further confusion about the definition of special education arose from the way the 1944 Act was interpreted in the early years. With the main emphasis being placed on the provision of separate day and boarding special schools, special education became equated with special schooling. Many of the administrative decisions made by local education authorities during the 1950s and 1960s implied that special education only existed in special schools. Ordinary schools, by definition, could not provide special education. Help for learning difficulties in primary and secondary schools thus became remedial education which drifted apart from special schooling. Separate services developed with different administrations and advisers, and the answer to the question 'What is Special Education?' became 'what happens in special schools'. Special schools were often preoccupied with techniques and therapies rather than curriculum development. In the case of hearing and visual impairment, methods and materials dominated discussion, in the case of those with physical disabilities, techniques and therapies, and in the case of emotional and behaviour disorders, regimes and therapies. Methodology also dominated special education teacher training and curriculum considerations were often limited to the acquisition of literacy. Like all brief summaries this can be challenged by specific examples which refute the general case, but it has only been since the early 1970s that the range and quality of the curricula offered in special schools has been a matter of active concern. There were many reasons for this concern, including attention to curriculum development in ordinary schools and the changing population of special schools, but perhaps one of the most potent stimuli was the integration movement.

The major challenge to traditional forms of special education stemmed from social concern about the isolation and marginalisation of those who were handicapped by separate provision. The movement towards greater participation in the ordinary range of community institutions gathered strength from trends outlined in the previous chapter. The concept of integration as a dynamic process is a difficult one to grasp. It is often confused with physical location and often discussed in terms of specific situations rather than in terms of the whole life-style of children and adults who are disabled.

The first effect of moves towards integration was the recognition that special education could no longer be equated with special schooling. Special education could be provided in ordinary schools. When people began to look at how children with disabilities might be educated in primary and secondary schools, the curriculum in the ordinary school became an important consideration. Comparisons had to be made between the curricula and as a result special schools began to make clearer statements about the curriculum they offered. The close scrutiny of the ordinary school programme to judge its appropriateness was accompanied by the recognition of much common ground between ordinary and special education, particularly with respect to less successful learners in the former. This reappraisal of the special school curriculum is usefully summarised in the Schools Council Report written by Mary Wilson 'The Curriculum in Special Schools'.[4]

To summarise this section, special education is no longer defined by where it takes place or by techniques appropriate to categories of handicap. It is no longer seen as a different and separate form of education. Above all, it is being defined in educational terms and not principally in terms of methods, treatments and therapies. Its definition is now closely related to the aims and objectives of the public education service as a whole.

The Ordinary School Context

Schools in recent years have been under pressure to improve standards and increase attention to a variety of special needs at a time of falling rolls and reduced resources. As a result of the 1981 Education Act they have also been required to give greater attention to the identification of and provision for special educational needs. It is necessary to look at the issue of improved standards and to relate consideration of special educational needs to other special needs which primary and secondary schools are expected to meet.

In an historic sense it was standards in ordinary schools which determined the need for special education in the case of the largest groups receiving it, namely, those in the categories of educationally subnormal and maladjustment. Although the change to comprehensive education resulted in many more administrators and teachers recognising the range of abilities and achievements to be expected in a school population, there still remain many politicians and educators who seek a basic standard of performance for the majority. The move from norm referenced attainments to criterion referenced assessment of individual progress is slow and halting. The recognition of individual differences and individual needs, although increasing, is not always very evident in the way schools work in practice.

In many developed countries there has been a reaction to comprehensive, liberal education and demands have been voiced for a return to 'basics' and for cutting out 'the clutter'. A search for higher standards and more effective schools has considerable implications for special education. These depend on how the search is carried out. On the one hand, it could result in a better matching of tasks, objectives and materials to individuals. On the other, it could result in a narrower common curriculum, a less flexible approach to individual needs and the stigmatisation of pupils as not up to standard. The former approach leads to special educational arrangements being seen as a variant of a number of different approaches to learning while the latter may characterise it as charitable provision for failures.

The central point, in discussing the improvement of general standards, is that the ordinary school programme is a potential creator of special educational needs. If the school is sensitive to the problems of less successful learners, if it takes steps within its organisation, methodology and curriculum to meet their needs, and if individual progress is emphasised rather than the achievement of norms and examination successes, the number of individuals whose learning difficulties become special educational needs may be mimimised. This whole school response to the needs of all pupils who attend it is of crucial importance to the discussion of special educational needs and provision.

The relationship of special educational needs to other special needs in schools is still the subject of some confusion with the terms used interchangeably in many instances. It is perhaps most helpful to see special needs as a general term and special educational needs as a specific example. This is necessary because the latter are now defined in the 1981 Education Act. A number of different groups within primary and secondary schools may have special needs to be taken into account when organising the work of the school and selecting objectives, methods and materials. These groups may include gifted children, children from ethnic minority groups, travellers children, socially disadvantaged children and children of service and mobile familities. They may need special consideration as individuals and as groups within the school's programme. Special educational needs, on the other hand, are clearly defined as learning difficulties significantly greater than those of the majority of children of the same age. Children with special needs may or may not have special educational needs.

The ordinary school context, its objectives, its priorities and its ethos, has a vital bearing on special education. Although disabilities and significant difficulties can be defined more or less precisely by medical, psychological, social and educational assessment, the need for special educational provision, which may result from them, remains relatively determined, that is, determined by the capacity of the ordinary school to recognise and meet a variety of individual special needs.

Current Concepts of Special Education

Having said that special education is no longer defined by location and suggested that the need for it is relatively defined in terms of the capacity of primary and secondary schools to respond to individual differences, it is nevertheless important to describe its main characteristics. There are a number of assumptions, based on research and experience, which underpin these characteristics and which may be summarised as follows:

(1) the needs of children with disabilities and difficulties are not different in nature from those of other children. There are not two sorts of children, those who are handicapped and those who are not. Children who may require special education have more general human needs in common with other children than they have different ones.

(2) disabilities and difficulties vary widely in nature and
     degree. There is a continuation from minor ones to severe
     and profound ones. The special educational needs which
     may arise from them vary over time and may be short- or
     long-term.

(3) the handicapping effects of disabilities and difficulties are
     individual and although they may be categorised in
     medical and psychological terms, the same categories do
     not define special educational needs. As a result children
     with disabilities and difficulties need individual assess-
     ment and individual statements of their needs and of how
     they might be met within the education service.

These assumptions are not only implicit in the criteria for
special educational needs and provision in the Warnock Report
but are also recognised in the arrangements made by other
countries. For example, in Norway recent legislation has

> established special education as a function of the compulsory
> school and as something which can, if necessary, be offered
> wherever a child resides. Special education is not provided for
> categories of children or handicapped children but for any child or
> youth who does not (temporarily or for a longer period) profit from
> ordinary education. The demand for special education will vary in
> extent and quality with the variations of ordinary education at any
> place or at any time.[3]

Similarly, in the United States, Public Law 94–142 requires that
children who are handicapped 'receive a free, appropriate public
education in the least restrictive educational environment . . . The
law further requires that the Individual Education Programme
will be the means of achieving provision in the least restrictive
environment and of meeting the unique needs of each child.'
These examples illustrate a general trend, linked with progress
towards integration, which individualises special educational
needs and provisions. It is a trend which recognises the limitations of categorical definitions, the changing perceptions of needs
and the need for special help in a wide variety of educational
situations.

The Warnock Report's criteria for special education are
threefold, namely: (i) effective access on a full or part-time basis to
teachers with appropriate qualifications or substantial experience
or both; (ii) effective access on a full or part-time basis to other
professionals with appropriate training; and (iii) an educational
and physical environment with the necessary aids, equipment
and resources appropriate to the child's special needs. These are

linked with three other characteristics which extend the third criterion, namely: (i) the provision of special means of access to the curriculum through special equipment, facilities or resources, modifications of the physical environment or special techniques; (ii) the provision of a special or modified curriculum; and (iii) particular attention to the social structure and emotional climate in which education takes place. The point about the curriculum is reinforced by the further statement that 'every attempt should be made to see that the chosen objectives (of the curriculum) are as near in scope and quality to those of other children of the same age as is practicable given the nature and degree of children's disabilities.'

Special education is thus concerned with teacher training, appropriate equipment and resources, appropriate curricula and appropriate teaching situations just like ordinary education. It is a variant of ordinary education, not a different kind of education. Just as special educational needs are relative, determined by the ability of ordinary schools to meet individual needs, special education is also relative. The definition of special education rests on the degree to which it makes modifications or provides support to individuals beyond what is practical and possible in the ordinary school.

Relativity is an important characteristic since it carries with it the implication that schools can become better at meeting different individual needs of all kinds. The better the ordinary system, the fewer the number of minor disabilities and difficulties which may require special educational provision. There is no set population for special education, nor any hard or fast criteria for special educational needs. Provision alternative to and different from that provided in ordinary classes, the 1981 Act definition of special education, will and should continue to change in nature with changes in ordinary education.

Special Education as a Service Delivery System

The change from an institutionally based model of provision to a more flexible range of arrangements in ordinary schools and elsewhere leads naturally to a service delivery model for special education. The new emphasis on individual assessment and individual programme planning also supports the trend to bring special education to children rather than take children to special education. The essential features of a service delivery model are the identification of the range of possible provisions in terms of levels of intervention and the planning of professional intervention as near to the ordinary classroom situation as possible.

Programmes for individuals with special educational needs have two major interrelated elements: an educational component and a related services component. The former includes the degree to which special education teachers intervene and the curriculum materials and equipment appropriate for the individual. The related services element includes non-teaching assistance, therapies and social welfare support.

The educational element centres on the curriculum. When this is the same as for other children it will primarily relate to the provision of special materials, for example, for blind students, or to the teaching methods necessary, for example, for hearing impaired students. Where it is different or varied, different elements may be taught in ordinary classes and elsewhere or it may all be taught in a separate educational situation.

The related services element is primarily enabling: the components facilitate personal development and thus education. Related services may include speech, physio- and occupational therapies, social welfare assistance and counselling and guidance. These services may or may not be the direct responsibility of education authorities but their delivery and coordination with the education element will be the responsibility of the education service.

The idea of service delivery and of the relationship between the two elements is illustrated by the following example. It is not suggested that this model is more widely applicable although it is effective in action and embodies important principles. In the USA the School Board of Madison, Wisconsin, has no separate special schools for children with physical and sensory disabilities or severe learning difficulties. It retains one or two alternative schools for behaviour-disordered students. Its special education arrangements are based on four levels of service delivery described as follows:[5]

Level 1　Regular education program with related services, non-academic activities with related services, extra curricular activities with related services. Characterised by consulting teacher, itinerant teacher options.

Level 2　Regular education program supplemented by exceptional educational program services at the resource level with related services, non-academic activities with related services, extra curricular activities with related services. Characterised by resource program option.

Level 3　Exceptional education with integration into regular education curriculum programs with related services, non-academic activities with related services, extra curricular activities with related services. Characterised by the self-contained integrated option.

Level 4 Exceptional education with related services, non-academic activities with related services, extra curricular activities with related services. Characterised by the self-contained option.

The development of individual programmes is based on the three elements, academic activities, non-academic activities and extra curricular activities. Provision is based on providing Level 1 services to all schools while Level 2, 3 and 4 services are provided in selected schools in each area of the city. Level 1 is primarily concerned with related services, whereas the other three levels include more and more special educational instruction in resource rooms or separate classes. Each individual when assessed is assigned to a level of service delivery which may be changed when progress is reviewed annually.

Variations of this idea of levels of service delivery are now relatively common in the United States as a result of their legislation and as a consequence of developing a range of provision to which individual education programmes can be related. The new arrangements for making statements in England and Wales also imply the development of levels of service, firstly, by the decision whether or not to make a statement, secondly, by making the curriculum a central feature of the education element and, thirdly, by separating educational and non-educational provision in the statement. Non-educational provision will include related services not provided by education authorities. In deciding on their pattern of special educational provision and on the level of interaction necessary for individuals as a result of assessment, it is suggested that the level of service delivery will become increasingly important as a major characteristic of special education.

Summary

Special education is now more closely linked to education for all not only because of progress towards integration but also because the determination of special educational needs is not simply based on the nature of an individual's disability or significant difficulty. These needs are now to be individually determined and will become evident in relation to the degree to which ordinary schools are responsible to individual differences in their general programme. Special education provision has now to be defined individually in educational terms, curriculum methods and in teaching skills rather than in institutional and categorical terms, and this suggests that a service delivery model based on levels and kinds of intervention is necessary.

CHAPTER 4

The Range of Needs and Provision

The Range of Needs

Up to now little has been said about the range of disabilities and difficulties which may give rise to special educational needs. Before looking at the elements in a range of provision it may be helpful to consider some characteristics of the population to be served. These characteristics have become more difficult to summarise as assessment methods have become more sophisticated. The following diagram is a starting point:

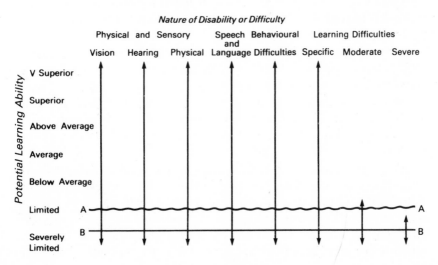

The left-hand column represents a range of potential learning abilities. It is intended as a description of the results of nature and nurture as assessed at any age and no more than that. The vertical lines, each linked to a particular disability, represent the range of potential learning ability which might be expected among the individuals with the disability but do not indicate the distribution of potential ability within those with the same disability. For example, some physical disabilities have associated learning difficulties and a high proportion of individuals with them may fall within the below average range. Finally, research has shown a significant percentage of individuals to have more than one disability or difficulty. For example, children with behaviour difficulties may have specific learning difficulties and children may have both physical and sensory disabilities and learning difficulties.

The two lines A and B represent another aspect which affects provision. The wavy line A represents a borderline between below average and significantly limited learning potential which in the past was taken as that between ordinary schooling and education in an ESN (M) special school. Currently it represents more of a curricular distinction between that for less successful pupils in ordinary schools and that provided for children with moderate learning difficulties in ordinary or special schools. The lower line B represents the approximate level below which an even more specialised curriculum is needed as in special schools for those with severe and profound learning difficulties.

The diagram illustrates some of the difficulties in making provision by the traditional approach according to disability categories. For example, if specialist teaching skills are necessary for children with vision, hearing and physical disabilities and also for teaching children with severely limited learning potential, and if specialist teaching is concentrated in special schools and classes for each disability, where are the children with physical and sensory disabilities below lines A and B to be placed? These difficulties are leading to the view that the kind of curriculum to be offered should be the major determinant of provision, with specialist teaching skills perhaps regrouped in different combinations.

One final point about the diagram is that it does not represent the relative sizes of the populations with different disabilities and difficulties. These are indicated in Table I (below). It should be remembered, however, that these figures indicate the number of children in special schools and special classes; they do not indicate the number of children receiving special help who are in

Table I
*Children in England and Wales Assessed to Need Special Educa-
tion in Special Schools, Special Classes and Awaiting Placement, 1
January 1982*

Disability	Number	Percentage
Blind	990	0.6
Partially Sighted	2,065	1.3
Deaf	3,387	2.1
Partially Hearing	4,261	2.7
Physically Handicapped	13,999	8.9
Delicate	4,691	4.0
Moderate Learning Difficulties	70,529	45.1
Severe Learning Difficulties	30,503	19.5
Maladjusted	21,442	37.1
Epileptic	975	0.6
Speech Defects	2,496	1.6
Autistic	1,028	0.7
Total	156,384	100.2

N.B.: Of these children 14,502, about nine per cent, were in special classes or
units in ordinary schools.

ordinary classes, nor do they indicate those children with physical
and sensory disabilities in schools for children with moderate and
severe learning difficulties.

The relative sizes of the groups represent a particular problem
for the development of provision when the policy is to minimise
residential special education and maximise day provision in
schools near children's homes. It is far easier to provide for small
incidence disabilities in boarding schools with a wide catchment
area than to disperse limited resources throughout a variety of
local arrangements.

The previous paragraphs are only intended as a background
sketch. The true nature of the range of special educational needs
and the individual combinations to be found in any area is not yet
known with any precision. Epidemiological studies related to
disabilities do not indicate special education needs, while current
placement policies remain conditioned by what is available. Only
when detailed assessments of individuals, of a similar kind to
those to be undertaken when making statements, are available in
large numbers will it be possible to have sufficient information on
which to plan an appropriate range of provision and services.
Meanwhile, the only practical steps are: to develop a special

education policy based on the general principles outlined in chapters 2 and 3; to reorganise and modify existing provision and services and make them compatible with the aims of the policy developed; and to evaluate the effectiveness of arrangements through the regular review of individual progress.

The Range of Provision

There have been a number of theoretical formulations of the range of provision, for example, those of Deno, Cope and Anderson,[8] and Gearhart and Weishahn,[9] which are discussed in Hegarty, Pocklington and Lucas.[2] It may, however, be most helpful to start from a brief description of all the forms of provision which are available now in this country and elsewhere. These descriptions can then be related to possible models, including levels of service delivery, and to different incidence and geographical variables. They have been confined to the compulsory school period. Pre- and post-school provision, which are equally important, will be dealt with in later sections.

1. *Provision wholly within the ordinary class or group*

This may take at least three different forms:

(a) *Interpretative and social assistance* The teacher is wholly responsible for the educational programme of all children within the class within the schools curriculum guidelines. He or she may be assisted by another adult full- or part-time.

   The first kind of assistance may be illustrated by considering certain kinds of physical disability which involve mobility and fine motor cordination difficulties and self-care problems. In such cases, where the child is capable of profiting from the educational programme, assistance may be given with moving round the school, setting up and supervising tasks involving assistance with the use of equipment and materials, and assistance with feeding, toileting and dressing and other self-care tasks. At best, this assistance should also involve training to increase independence.

   Interpretation may be needed in the case of hearing impaired children. For example, in a classroom in the USA hearing impaired pupils, who had responded to a total communication approach, were assisted by an interpreter who transmitted the teacher's instructions, clarified questions and generally ensured that the disabled pupils could participate as fully as possible. Finally, aides in the classroom, under the teacher's direction, can give individual attention to the practical of learning tasks so that these are properly mastered. A service is thus provided which supplements that of the class teacher, giving extra attention to the individual with a disability.

(b) *Consultancy* Again the class teacher is wholly responsible for the work of the class but, in this case, he or she is assisted by a visiting special education teacher. The visits may vary in frequency depending on the assessed needs of the child. They may also be for a variety of purposes including helping the class teacher to understand the child's disability, joint planning with the class teacher of learning tasks, the provision of special materials for learning, counselling and supporting the individual child, and assessing his or her progress. The visiting teacher provides specialist support to the teacher and child and is a resource available to the class teacher.

(c) *Co-teaching* This is a relatively recent development but one which offers great advantages when it is effectively carried out. Responsibility for children with special educational needs is shared, not only in respect of planning educational activities, but also in teaching. Co-teaching and collaborative teaching can take two forms. In the first instance the special education teacher may spend programmed time working in the ordinary class. The second instance is a form of team teaching where a special education teacher works full-time with ordinary teachers as part of a team responsible for a group of children.

The first form of co-teaching involves the special education teacher being in the ordinary primary class for set periods each week or working with particular subject teachers in secondary schools. The two teachers plan the class activities and share teaching, with the special educator concentrating on work with those children identified as having learning difficulties. This form of teaching is currently being practiced as part of the policy of the Grampian region of Scotland.

Collaborative teaching as a form of team teaching is perhaps less common. It was promoted within the Swedish school system in the late 1970s as an answer to learning difficulties of all kinds. The main idea was that three teachers, including one with a special education background would be responsible for a group of children equal in size to about three classes. They would be free to organise sub-groupings flexibly and use their time to meet special educational needs within the total programme by co-teaching and collaboration. This approach is inherent in other forms of team teaching but it is less common to have a special educator as a full member of the team.

2. *Provision additional to education within the ordinary class*

This may also take three distinct forms and may be combined with any of the three kinds of arrangement described in the previous section.

(a) *Additional special teaching* Often this is based on a resource centre but may take place in any situation where the special education teacher withdraws individuals or small groups from ordinary classes. The special educator may be a member of the school staff or a visiting teacher from a peripatetic service. Such special teaching may take three broad forms: technical instruction, alternative curriculum studies, or activities designed to ameliorate emotional and behaviour difficulties. Among the activities described as technical instruction might be language work with the hearing-impaired, or programmes for children with specific learning difficulties. These may include reading, writing and spelling where these are not taught in ordinary classes with or without co-teaching assistance. The alternative curriculum studies might include typing skills for children unable to write, or learning skills and replacements for inappropriate elements of the ordinary class programme, for example, a second language in some secondary schools. The third form would be characterised by the teacher providing a social climate and programme designed to mitigate emotional and behaviour problems and to support individuals in their relationships with others in ordinary classes.

(b) *Therapies* Where children are assessed to need, for example, speech and physiotherapy as part of their programme to meet special educational needs, these may be provided in addition to the arrangements in the previous sections. Regular sessions with therapists may be provided in their own schools or they may need to attend health service clinics.

(c) *Attendance at classes, centres and special schools outside the ordinary school* This form of special education may involve the individual in attendance at a child guidance centre, sessions spent in units specialising in their disabilities or part-time attendance at a special school. It may be provided for children with specific learning difficulties, behaviour difficulties and other disabilities. While most frequently provided on a sessional basis each week it is sometimes provided on a short course basis. For example, in Sweden and Denmark visually handicapped students attending primary schools may regularly attend special schools for block periods of instruction each year.

3. *Special classes and units in ordinary schools*

Where there are sufficient children with similar needs in one school, or where a local education authority decides to concentrate such a group in a particular school, a special class may be set up. In this case the primary responsibility for the education programme rests with the special class teacher. Such classes may be part-time with individuals attending ordinary classes for some elements of the curriculum or full-time when the teacher provides the whole curriculum.

The term unit is sometimes used to refer to special classes but it more properly refers to groups of classes for the same disability set up within schools. Special classes and units may also have therapists who work with teachers on a regular basis, as in arrangements for children with speech and language disorders.

4. *Separate special units*

A variety of special units have been set up by education authorities, usually where it is hoped that special educational needs will be relatively short-term or where it is thought necessary to assess pupils in a different environment. These units do not have all the facilities of schools, ordinary or special, and they are usually intended to provide short periods of intensive assessment and special education. Among the disabilities and difficulties for which they have been set up are serious learning difficulties (remedial centres) and behaviour problems.

5. *Day special schools*

Day special schools have always concentrated on more severe and complex long-term special educational needs. Originally intended to deal with a single category of handicap, their population is now more mixed. Progress towards integration has challenged their original purposes and their current functions are under review. At one time they were seen as providing a long-term alternative to ordinary schools, and children, once ascertained as requiring them, attended for their whole school career. The situation has now changed and many provide short-term help with the aim of preparing some individuals to attend ordinary schools. A number provide part-time special education for pupils who also attend regular sessions in ordinary schools.

6. Boarding special schools

Residential education was originally provided for children with physical and sensory disabilities. Boarding schools were a means of providing the special education necessary which could not be provided in the child's home area. Later such schools were also set up for children with moderate learning difficulties either because they lived in a rural area or because their home circumstances were considered to contribute to their problems. More recently, boarding schools were seen as an essential form of provision for maladjusted children whose emotional and behaviour problems may not respond to other forms of help. The development of the kinds of arrangement already described has influenced the work of boarding schools.

7. Education in other institutions

Special education services have been responsible in many countries, including the United Kingdom, for educational arrangements in hospital and homes and centres for children in care. Provision in hospitals is broadly of two kinds, special help in ordinary hospitals for children of school age undergoing relatively short-term or intermittent treatment, and education for children spending longer periods in psychiatric and mental handicap hospitals. In many hospitals there are special schools and in others teaching units of different sizes. Similarly, teaching services are provided in some larger children's homes and in observation and assessment centres.

8. Education at home

Education at home is an important element in pre-school provision but this will be dealt with in that context. For children of school age, home teaching is normally provided for periods when illness or accident prevent school attendance. In recent years it has also been provided for children awaiting places in special schools and for those whose emotional and behaviour problems make them unable to attend school or unacceptable to schools.

Summary

A range of special educational arrangements has been briefly described and further discussion of issues associated with elements in the range occurs in chapter 6. All the elements exist but in relatively few instances do they form a coherent pattern of special educational provision. The range can be looked at from an historical perspective and from a theoretical standpoint.

Some research workers, including those cited earlier, have attempted to rationalise the range as a continuous or cascade system. The range is characterised by a decrease in incidence and an increase in the complexity of learning difficulties from sections 1 to 8. Others, adopting an integration philosophy, draw the lines of what is acceptable at different points in the range. In practice, each element has come into being to meet a particular need or as an individual pioneering effort. The theories tend to systematise the existing provision.

CHAPTER 5

The Extended Range of Provision

Up to this point little has been said about the parents of children with disabilities and significant difficulties. Often in the past they have been expected to be the passive receivers of professional advice and onlookers of their children's education. Now their contribution to education is recognised as vital, particularly in the pre-school years. Parents of children with disabilities and significant learning difficulties have been active in campaigning for better pre- and post-school provision and in seeking an active role in their children's education. Initiatives to accept parents as partners have been recognised in the greater weight given to parental views and wishes in the 1981 Education Act.

Most parents of children with disabilities and significant difficulties have at least two major concerns. In the early months and years they want to know what to do to minimise the handicapping effects of the disabilities and to enhance the growth and development of their children. From the teenage years onwards their concerns change to a preoccupation with what sort of life their children can lead as adults, particularly when parental support may no longer be available. These two areas of concern have provided an important stimulus to the development of pre- and post-school arrangements.

Equally important has been the work of professionals in health, psychological and educational research and development. Child development studies have emphasised the importance of early intervention to reduce handicapping effects. Similarly, at the other end of the compulsory school period, the importance of continuing programmes, particularly in social and life skills, has been demonstrated. Educational programmes need to be continued and extended if individuals with more severe special educational needs are to lead an effective, worthwhile and independent life.

Pre-school Provision

It is not proposed to argue the case for early intervention as its value is now a matter of fact. However, two points might be made before considering the current range of provision. The first is concerned with discovery and diagnosis. The second concerns the nature of education during this phase.

Only the most severe and obvious visual, hearing, physical and intellectual disabilities are easily discovered at or soon after birth. The less obvious and less severe developmental disabilities will only emerge during the early years and some only when education begins. Discovery will depend on the effectiveness of child health services, the alertness and interest of parents and general practitioners, and the skill of paediatric assessment centres when babies and young children are referred to them. The prevention of or mitigation of handicapping effects may depend on an adequate system of developmental assessment in the early years as well as on parents' understanding of child development and their conscientiousness in seeking advice. Both these developments will be inadequate if they are not associated with counselling, guidance, early therapy and early education programmes.

Although kindergarten and nursery education has a long history it has only been available in most instances from the age of three. Indeed, when discussing the provisions of the 1981 Education Act, it was necessary to argue that education was possible below the age of two years. This discussion was necessary because of the traditional view of education as being merely a formal acquisition of knowledge and skills in a classroom. Defined in this way, education from the early months was inconceivable and considered not to be possible. However, once it was accepted that education should be characterised by planned experiences and mediation in terms of the definition given in chapter 3, it then became possible to see that from the early months, parents and other adults can plan and carry out a systematic programme of activities of an educational kind. This kind of intervention did not arise only from theoretical considerations. Early work with the hearing and the visually impaired had demonstrated the value of building on residual hearing and vision to establish communication, and of providing alternative experiences. This made the case for pre-school education programmes and was followed by similar arrangements for young children with physical disabilities and severe degrees of mental retardation.

All disciplines which contribute to child development now recognise the astonishing rate of change and growth during the first three years and the importance of making appropriate provision for mitigating as much as possible the potentially serious effects of disabilities during those years. Thus pre-school provision rests on two important prerequisites, an adequate health and development surveillance system during the first three years, and the development of effective intervention programmes which, at least in the early stages, can be managed by parents with the help of visiting professionals.

The responsibility for seeking early special educational help rests firstly with parents although they have no legal duty to ensure that their children are educated before reaching the age of five. However, the DES Circular 1/83 has placed a wider obligation on local education authorities to ensure that adequate provision is made for *all* children with special educational needs; and under Section 6 of the Education Act children under the age of two may be assessed by the LEA if the parents agree and *must* be assessed if the parents present a reasonable case. This means that for children under two and, by implication at least, for all pre-school children, the LEA shares responsibility with the parents.

Current provision has risen in an *ad hoc* way with services more readily available for some disabilities, for example, hearing impairment, than others. Local education authorities have not always wanted to be asked to make pre-school provision, although some have been very active in developing early intervention programmes. Under the new legislation they will have to agree to reasonable requests for assessments and respond positively if special educational needs are revealed. In times of limited resources, however, persuasive arguments and evidence will be required before comprehensive services are planned. There is, nevertheless, a compelling case for better provision in the early years.

Kinds of Pre-School Provision

The importance of discovery, diagnosis and assessment has already been mentioned. This is not the context to discuss the important work of hospital-based or other kinds of community health services; the kinds of provision discussed in this section will be those made by education services in conjunction with other services. Before turning to the range of possibilities, one point needs to be made about assessment. This is that for some children, whose disabilities and developmental delays are not easily diagnosed, assessment should take place over time. For them a taught programme may be necessary to estimate learning potential and clarify the nature of learning difficulties. Any of the elements of pre-school provision may have an assessment function as well as an educational one.

Home visiting teaching

This form of arrangement involves regular visits to the child's home with the special education teacher working with the child, deciding with the parents a programme of activities to be carried out between visits, and helping parents to acquire the necessary techniques to help the child learn. Such services are normally provided for children with severe degrees of hearing and visual disabilities and for severe mental retardation. Where services are well developed they may be provided for a wider range of developmental problems including disadvantaged home circumstances as was the case in the original Portage programme in the United States.

The Portage material, which has been tested out in England in the Wessex Hospital Region, is now used more widely. It is significant in two respects. First, it is a planned sequence of activities in major areas of a child's development. The teacher, and more particularly the parents, have some choice in which activity to develop with their children from week to week. Secondly, because the material is carefully planned, a number of differently qualified or experienced adults can work with parents under the supervision of a support group of psychologists and teachers. Because of its structure it extends the range of potential educators.

There are other similar materials available all of which raise an interesting question about the sharing of expertise. The first home teaching services of this kind for the hearing impaired relied on qualified teachers of the deaf who used their expertise directly, devising individual programmes on a one-off basis in each home. The Portage approach puts similar expertise in a form which can be used by others, including parents, with the minimum specialist training, provided there is a back-up group of more qualified professionals to supervise the service. There are many potential educators of the young child, but the parents are the most important. There are unlikely to be sufficiently highly skilled special education teachers to provide a direct service to all the families who need it and hence one promising way forward is the development of special education programmes for others to use.

Other peripatetic teaching

There are at least two other situations where peripatetic teaching services for young children with special educational needs may operate. These are day nurseries run by social service departments and playgroups. The priorities for admission to day nurseries are such that a significant proportion of children who attend them may be expected to have special educational needs at some time in their school career. It is now possible for special education teachers with responsibilities for young children to work in these nurseries and to provide support to staff where children have obvious physical and sensory disabilities.

Play groups supervised by social service departments also accept children with disabilities. Some, such as those described as opportunity groups, make a particular effort both to integrate children considered handicapped with others of the same age and to provide specialist therapies and learning programmes. Special education teachers can be an important resource available to play groups.

Nursery schools and units

Nursery education, which can be provided in nursery schools from the age of two and in nursery classes classes from the age of three, is of considerable value to all children. However, it is not widespread. The Warnock Report noted that in 1977 it was only available to 0.5 per cent of two-year-olds, 15.3 per cent of three-year-olds and 14.9 per cent of four-year-olds. These figures are unlikely to have increased in recent years. For young children with special educational needs there are two possibilities, either attendance at an ordinary nursery school or unit, if available, or attendance at a special unit usually attached to a special school. A survey of sixty-one nursery facilities was carried out by HM Inspectorate during 1981–82 and the report,[10] published in 1983, gives useful information about the current situation.

(a) *Ordinary nursery schools and units* The majority of these cater for a wide range of children including those with special needs. In a minority of cases the school or unit may include a special class of children with the same disability. A significant minority of all children attending these schools and units have identified special educational needs, many discovered before admission.

The advantages of this kind of arrangement are that the child with a disability or significant difficulty can attend the local nursery with other children in the neighbourhood; during the programme there is exposure to a wide range of ordinary models of behaviour and the process of integration can be encouraged from the earliest age. The balance of structured and exploratory experiences normally caters for different interests and levels of development and can include many children with special educational needs without distortion. However, unless staffing, facilities and resources take into account the presence of such children, there can be disadvantages. Activities and programmes to meet specific needs may not be possible and staff may not be able to give them sufficient time. Also, if specialist teaching advice is not available, programmes may lack rigour and effectiveness.

(b) *Nursery units in special schools* One reason for this provision is that young children can not only receive appropriate special education but they can also profit from the range of therapies available at the schools which are not normally available in ordinary provision. Individual programmes can be developed based on a curriculum with continuity into education in the school. Children can make an early start on a long-term special education programme which, if effective, may enable them to attend ordinary schools later in their school career. Conversely, it may be argued, they enter a separate situation with little contact with other children of their own age and the process of integration may be inhibited.

(c) *Special nursery units in ordinary schools* Although less common, such arrangements would seem to offer the advantages of both previous forms of arrangement and have fewer disadvantages. This is perhaps the most common pre-school arrangement for those who are mentally handicapped in Sweden. Within an ordinary children's centre there are special class bases and special staff for each group. From these bases they go out individually and as a group, often with teachers, to take part in planned activities with other children. They attend an ordinary local facility within which special arrangements are made for them.

This brief review of pre-school provision would not be complete without stressing again that it is in this phase in particular that health, social and education services, together with voluntary agencies and parents, all make a contribution. Provision remains patchy and contributions are not usually well coordinated. It remains difficult to get those not directly involved with pre-school children to give this phase a high enough priority and sufficient resources. ⫽

Post-compulsory School Provision

It is only recently that the tradition of post-compulsory school education solely for the academically able has been challenged. Further education colleges have been preoccupied, until the past decade, with further academic and technical qualifications. At sixteen most less successful achievers in secondary schools were expected to leave school and find work. The same pattern of expectation was evident in special education with a minority of those with physical and sensory disabilities going on to higher and further education and the majority leaving school to go to work, attend training and day centres or remain at home or in institutions. Some forty per cent of all school leavers had no further education after the compulsory school period.

Since the mid-1970s, however, the position has changed. The recommendations of the Warnock Report, together with parental pressure, have stimulated the development of provision in schools and colleges and re-established the right to education up to the age of nineteen. More recently, the Further Education Unit has reviewed and disseminated good practice. As a result, more young people deemed handicapped have been staying on in school, attending colleges of further education and special colleges set up to meet their needs. It is important to note that the same constraints on development exist as for pre-school provision, namely, that parents have to ask for provision. Although some local education authorities have taken positive steps to provide courses in the 16–19 age range, many still reluctantly respond to parental pressure. At a time of limited resources this may be understandable, but it remains a matter of considerable regret that continuing education, often vital for the successful transition to adult and working live for those who are handicapped, has to rely on pressure groups for its development.

The rather grudging admission of the importance and value of a longer period of education is in stark contrast to the approach in other countries. In Sweden and Norway between eighty and ninety per cent of all young people, including those considered handicapped, remain in Upper Secondary schools to the age of seventeen and beyond. In Sweden the Board of Education is responsible for provision, in school or elsewhere, for all young people up to the age of nineteen. Legislation in the United States entitles young people who are handicapped to education in high schools or elsewhere up to the age of twenty-one.

The transition from school to adult and working life is an important phase in the lives of all young people, particularly those with disabilities and significant difficulties. Some of the important issues related to it will be discussed in a later chapter. Transition is a phase in which many departments and agencies play a part. Ministries of Health, Social Services, Education and Employment may all make some form of provision. At this point we shall discuss the elements in the range of possibilities for which the education service may be responsible.

Staying on in Ordinary Schools

Some children with disabilities, who have made reasonable progress with support in ordinary schools, may stay on with their contemporaries in VIth forms to take examinations and other courses. The advantages in such cases are that specialist subject teaching is readily available, access routes to higher and further education are well known, and young people are likely to be conscientiously prepared for examinations. There are, however, some disadvantages which may arise from a lack of specific attention to personal and social needs. For example, a disability such as blindness may not limit academic success, if supporting materials and services are readily provided, but the disability may be much more handicapping when seeking employment. Ordinary schools need to know about future prospects as well as current special educational needs. Similarly, many individuals with disabilities need special counselling and training programmes to acquire social and life skills to minimise the handicapping effects of their conditions. Most ordinary schools have neither the expertise nor the time to provide such help for individuals. Staying on in ordinary schools can be successful if the academic programme is supplemented by other arrangements but, because individuals are seen to cope with the lessons, other transition needs may be forgotten.

Staying on in Special Schools

Some special schools for those with physical and sensory disabilities have had a tradition of providing academic VI form courses. More recently, others have retained pupils to complete 16-plus examinations at an older age. Although there has been an increase in the number of young people who are handicapped taking the traditional route to some kind of academic qualification, another trend is becoming evident. Young people with moderate and severe degrees of mental retardation are also now staying on in special schools.

For those in the moderate group the main stimulus has been either late entry to special schools or the absence of paid employment. Where an additional year is seen as helpful to the individual, so that he can complete more successfully the school's leaving programme, staying on can be valuable. There is more doubt about whether the special school is the best setting for a 16–19 programme of further education. Many favour a change of scene to the college of further education, where the ambience encourages a more mature pattern of social interaction. Nevertheless, one option which now exists is a post-16 course in a special school. Where this is well planned in a relatively self-contained base which creates greater and more relevant demands it can be a successful element in transition.

The position is slightly different in schools for those with severe degrees of mental retardation. Two major trends have been evident. Firstly, research and experience has demonstrated the value of a longer period of education which many now feel should extend into the early twenties. Secondly, parents have been strong supporters of a longer period and, in many instances, do not see adult training centres in their present form as educational establishments. Some of the same reservations about staying on in school for the moderate group apply to those with severe disabilities, often with more force. Because these children may enter an all-age school from the ages of two to five years, they may profit from a change of environment at sixteen. This consideration has resulted in some local education authorities setting up 2–14 and 14–19 schools. Where this has occurred, and the 14–19 curriculum is well planned, there are fewer objections to staying on in school. Other authorities have set up full- or part-time courses in colleges of further education and voluntary organisations have set up post-16 colleges. Some young people will benefit from taking a longer time to complete the curriculum up to sixteen. For many, however, the value of staying on in the special school will depend on the development of a separate 16–19 group with a specifically devised programme.

Thus, staying on in special schools of all kinds is an option to be considered first of all from the point of view of the individual's needs when an extended period to respond to the programme up to sixteen is recommended. Secondly, it is one form of 16–19 provision which can be made for the age group in the premises of a special school. This second option requires considerable planning if it is not to become simply a holding action to delay entry to employment or training or to avoid staying on at home without provision. Much depends on a careful selection of objectives and a well-planned programme.

Provision in Ordinary Colleges of Further Education

There has been a steady increase in the number of special arrangements made in colleges. Three main forms have developed: supporting services to enable individuals to follow any of the regular courses available in the colleges; bridging courses to prepare individuals for entry into regular courses; and special courses designed to improve personal and social skills and employability. In addition, some colleges accept students part-time from schools and training centres for particular activities or provide staff to provide an educational input in other centres.

The commonest form of arrangement appears to be the one-year or two-year separate course aimed at work preparation, and the Further Education Unit has done valuable work in evaluating them. The advantages of this element in the range of provision are that young people who are handicapped are in a college with their contemporaries, they are expected to develop more mature behaviour and they have access to a wider range of social and vocational possibilities. Provided they have support, when necessary, from specialist teachers a period in a college can provide an important half-way stage to adult and working life. Even in the absence of work it can help to develop autonomy and a range of interests.

Provision in Special Colleges

There has been a steady increase in separate institutions which provide post-16 education and training. On the positive side such colleges have expertise in the disability for which they cater. They create a more adult pattern of living and their programmes include regular experience in the local community. One drawback is that the majority are residential. Residential experience may be of positive value to many young people who have remained at home until this stage, but experiences away from the home area may not always be relevant. To join in a rural community when one lives in a major city may not be the most appropriate experience for those who have to return to live there. Nevertheless, special colleges have an important part to play in a range of provision for all kinds of disabilities.

A discussion of education services would be incomplete without some reference to the youth service. This service has also been responsive to the needs of young people who are handicapped. Together with voluntary organisations which have developed clubs many local authorities have encouraged their youth services to cater for young disabled people. The variety of activities in clubs and centres encourages integration and develops social skills and interests thus making an important contribution during the transition period.

Post-18 Provision

There are two other elements providing for young adults who are disabled, namely, higher education and adult education. Many universities and colleges have taken steps to develop a policy for the admission of students who are handicapped and provide necessary support. For those not able to attend these institutions, the Open University has an outstanding record in helping disabled students to follow academic courses.

Adult education services have also increased their contribution either by providing courses in institutions or by making arrangements in their own centres to see that there is access to regular courses or to provide special ones. In this connection adult literacy and numeracy arrangements have had a considerable impact as has the BBC's initiatives such as 'On the Move' and 'Let's Go'.

This relatively brief review of pre-school and post-school arrangements illustrates that the last two or three decades have seen a marked extension in the age range covered by services in the education sector for children, young people and adults who are deemed to be handicapped. The elements of successful arrangements are now known and exist, but the priority given to them varies and their availability in particular areas is by no means certain. Some have to be provided, others depend on demand but all are important in ensuring a good base on which to establish principles of special education provision.

CHAPTER 6

Major Issues in Special Education

Having described a range of provision made by education services in chapter 4, this chapter discusses a number of issues which arise in making such arrangements. It is divided into five main sections: assessment; provision in primary and secondary schools; special schools and units; peripatetic services; and continuity. Continuity includes important aspects of movement from one phase of education to another and between elements in the range of provision within the same age group.

Assessment

The most significant change which has taken place in the assessment of children with disabilities and significant difficulties is from a system which placed children in categories of handicap to one based on determining individual special educational needs and specifying the means of meeting them. Although most clearly defined in the field of special education, this move away from categories is also evident in primary and secondary education. There is increasing recognition that recording achievements by norm referenced gradings does not give sufficient information about individual progress. More use is now being made of checklists of individual skills and knowledge, while considerable attention is being focused on individual records of experience and achievement and on pupil profiles in secondary schools and further education.

Individual assessment is becoming more widely recognised as a necessary basis on which to plan teaching objectives. This change in the ordinary school is an important starting point for assessing special educational needs. The better a school's system for assessing and recording the progress of all children, the easier it will be to build on additional procedures for determining the special educational needs of those with significant learning difficulties of all kinds. This is a further example of the close interaction between ordinary and special education and of the need for ordinary and special education teachers to plan assessment and record procedures in close cooperation.

Building on a school's assessment procedure for all children, the Warnock Report suggested five levels or stages for determining and meeting special educational needs. These have been endorsed in the guidance given in the 1981 Education Act. They are worth restating:

(a) the collection of available information by the class teachers and head teacher, discussion with parents about the learning difficulties experienced and an exploration of the ways in which needs might be met within the school's existing resources and arrangements;

(b) an assessment added to (a) by a special education teacher either on the school staff or from a visiting service, together with a search for possible solutions within the school including help from the special education teacher where appropriate;

(c) an assessment added to (a) or (b) by a visiting specialist available to the school, such as the school doctor, school nurse, educational psychologist, social worker, etc. A decision at this stage would include both seeking solutions within the school, adding special help from the professional concerned or referral for multi-professional assessment;

(d) multi-professional assessment to include as a minimum, medical, psychological and educational components; also to include other relevant professionals, particularly social workers, with a view to deciding whether to make a statement of special educational needs in accordance with the 1981 Education Act or whether to suggest alternative arrangements not requiring a statement;

(e) multi-professional assessment centres to be established to deal with specific, severe and complex problems similar in scope to (d) but more specialised.

Obviously the stages or levels are only differentiated for exposition and are not intended to be gone through slavishly. In practice, (a) and (b) might be telescoped and it might be decided to proceed from (a) to (c) or (d) directly without the intervening stages. The principle, however, is important because it first emphasises the need to look for solutions within the child's school and only secondly brings in outside expertise and alternatives. It stresses the importance of a school's knowledge and experience of the child, building on that experience and making minimum use of scarce professional expertise in the early stages.

There are a number of important consequences of this approach which have to be recognised. The first is that skills in simple techniques of assessment and programme planning have to be developed in every school. This requires special education teachers, educational psychologists and other specialists to provide techniques and help the class, subject and head teachers to become practised in their use. These procedures should not only identify the more common learning difficulties and the means of meeting them in the schools but also reveal more complex problems requiring detailed examination.

It will also be necessary for schools to work out with visiting specialists reasonable criteria for determining the special educational needs which can reasonably be met by the school's own provision. Although the early stages of assessment should reveal special educational needs, they should have another purpose. They should also inform the school about the effectiveness of its general approach to less successful learners. The more special needs that are revealed, the greater is the need for the school to review its ordinary curriculum and methodology for these pupils. It is often the case that special educational needs are actually being created by an inappropriate response to individual differences within the general teaching programme of the school.

A second set of criteria needs to be developed by local education authorities to indentify the smaller group of children with special educational needs who may need multi-professional assessment. Schools need guidance, and visiting professionals need to develop a reasonably consistent approach so that relatively simple problems are not referred before school based solutions have been sought and in order that children with serious needs are referred early enough for intervention to be effective. For some children whose learning difficulties are obscure, information about past performance, tests and clinic interviews may be insufficient. Assessment needs to take place in a special teaching situation where problems can be illuminated by a planned programme to explore the child's response to a variety of experiences. Temporary placement in a special school or unit may be necessary.

Thus, the major assessment issues are: how to develop the necessary skills in primary and secondary schools to make the best use of scarce specialist resources; how to develop reasonable criteria for the wider group of special educational needs and for deciding who needs full assessment; and how to ensure that the assessment of these needs is not divorced from a school's assessment procedures for all children. It is also necessary to review the total population revealed by assessment procedures in two contrasting ways. First, it is important to see whether the size of the group could be reduced by appropriate measures to modify the school's general approach to less successful learners. Secondly, it is essential as a means of evaluating the appropriateness of special educational arrangements in ordinary schools and elsewhere. The important change in emphasis to individual assessment and individually determined special educational provision should not lead to the neglect of the conditions which may give rise to special educational needs or of a constant reappraisal of the range of provision to meet them.

Special Education in Ordinary Schools

A variety of possible special educational arrangements in primary and secondary schools was described in chapter 4. There are many uncertainties about such provision, each requiring discussion by the education authority, its special educational services and individual schools to produce practical solutions. This discussion requires both a conceptual framework and a recognition of the nature of special educational needs. It is to these issues that the following sections are devoted.

What is it?

The first question to be considered is the purpose of special educational arrangements in ordinary schools. One common answer is to meet assessed special educational needs but this does not go far enough. To put it crudely, many schools in the past made remedial and other arrangements with two needs in view. Learning difficulties would either be cured or children with them would be taken out of circulation to avoid disrupting ordinary children. These purposes still exist and, because some special needs are transitory, it is not unreasonable to expect cures. Neither is it unrealistic to accept that some children may need a period in a separate group provided the general ethos of the school is an accepting one and social interaction with others is planned and developed. Problems arise because many schools either plan provision on the curing assumption or on the segregation assumption. Only recently have many recognised the need for a combination of short-term and long-term arrangements. New legislation and current knowledge have redefined the purpose of special education in ordinary schools and progress towards integration has reinforced this new formulation. The aim of special educational arrangements in ordinary schools is to maintain in the school as many children as possible with disabilities and significant difficulties by providing various combinations of personal support to individual children and their teachers, special materials and special teaching. The arrangements made to achieve this purpose should be flexible and should include both short- and long-term measures. They should be characterised by close collaboration between ordinary and special educational teachers. The ordinary school can no longer take measures to cure short-term difficulties while expecting long-term ones to be solved elsewhere.

A conceptual framework

Before turning to a discussion of the kinds of special educational arrangements which can be made by ordinary schools it may be helpful to consider a framework within which to set them, a framework which takes into account the relative nature of special educational needs and the new duties of schools which result from the 1981 Education Act. It is suggested that there are three interrelated aspects of a school's work. These are:

(a) *The whole school approach* Within the planning of the school's programme, its organisation, curriculum, methodology and its social objectives, provision will need to be made for less successful learners. The allocation of resources, teachers, materials and facilities to below average achievers is one aspect of the whole school approach. Another is the modifications of the curriculum, including the objectives chosen and the methods used to develop appropriate courses for less successful learners. This is an aspect of the work of the school as a whole which has a profound influence on the other two aspects which follow.

(b) *The school's special education response* This aspect of a school's work involves the discovery and assessment of special educational needs and provision for them. A school, with the help of visiting professionals, will need to decide on its own criteria. These will depend on the effectiveness of the whole school approach to less successful learners. Assessment will include supplementing the school's normal assessment and record-keeping system and provision may include a selection of the approaches outlined in chapter 4.

(c)   *The local education authority's special educational provision*   In order to meet the needs of children who are the subject of statements, or to supplement an ordinary school's resources in other ways, the local education authority may make special educational provision in ordinary schools. Such provision may include special supporting arrangements for individuals in ordinary classes and special classes and units for different combinations of special educational needs. Although this provision will supplement the school's normal resources, it will be important to see that it is also integrated into the school.

The relationship between these three aspects is an important and flexible one. The more effective (a), the less the need for (b), and the more effective (b), the less the need for (c). It is also vital to recognise that assessments made in the context of the school's special educational response should not only lead to provision for individuals but should also be used as an evaluation of one aspect of the whole school response. The more needs that are detected as part of the school's investigation of learning difficulties, the greater the importance of reappraising its ordinary programme for less successful learners.

One important consequence of this framework is that special educational arrangements should be an important item on the agenda of senior management in schools. The arrangements should be an integral part of a school's pattern of organisation and not just an added feature when resources allow. Special education is now one of a number of equal priorities, including other special needs, which should ensure, to the best possible extent, that all children get an appropriate programme and a fair share of resources. This may be difficult to accomplish because for many years head teachers of primary and secondary schools have been encouraged to think that special education only took place elsewhere.

Having made a general statement and outlined a conceptual

framework the next question is what constitutes a school's special education response. How is the legal definition of provision additional to, or different from, that available to the majority of children of the same age to be interpreted. It has already been shown that special educational needs are relatively determined and, as a result, they can only be precisely determined in each school. Similarly, although general guidance can be given, only the individual school can decide which forms of provision fit its organisation and deployment of resources. However, it is necessary to consider what forms of arrangement may reasonably be described as special educational provision before discussing them.

Some arrangements are relatively clear cut. For example, when a special education teacher works with a colleague within the ordinary class or withdraws individuals and small groups for extra help, something additional is being provided. Similarly, a special class set up by the school, taught full- or part-time by a special education teacher, is a clear example of alternative provision. There are, however, more confused situations. For instance, if a special class is taught by a teacher without special educational training or experience, does it provide special education? Where a secondary school streams or groups its pupils and keeps classes or groups for less successful learners as small as possible, and a special education teacher takes such groups, is special education provided or is it part of the school's response to the needs of less successful learners in its ordinary programme? The answers to these questions will be locally determined. The point in raising them is to note that a school's special education response is not always easy to define.

A second difficulty occurs in determining which children are receiving special education as a result of the work of special education peripatetic teachers. Their employment by the local education authority is clearly part of its special educational provision. Some of these teachers, for example those concerned with physical and sensory disabilities, may know of a large number of children with less severe disabilities in ordinary schools. The service they provide may be important in preventing special educational needs arising. Similarly, they may be available to support teachers and make visits to review individual progress. Only some of the children known may receive regular visits, including counselling and instruction and the provision of equipment and materials. Only these could be said to be receiving special education in the strictest sense.

Coordination and collaboration

Where children are supported in ordinary classes, or withdrawn from them for additional help, a number of common difficulties arise. Some are due to traditional working practices and some due to lack of training, a topic which will be discussed in a later chapter. Problems occur in nearly all schools and some of these, particular to secondary schools, will be discussed later.

Co-teaching

Starting from the least common, but in many ways most promising, provision, namely, additional help in the ordinary classroom, it is possible to identify a number of problem areas. When individual teachers have been used to having a class to themselves it is often difficult for them to accept another teacher in the same room. This may be due to a fear of exposure of their work to another, since teaching has been traditionally a private business conducted by one person behind closed doors. It also stems from the fact that teachers and others judge the progress of children in a class as a measure of teaching skill, and individuals feel a strong sense of responsibility for their own classes. Finally, the introduction of a second teacher may give rise to problems of adult relationships, clashes of personalities, difficulties in sharing relationships with children, and different styles of teaching.

Given that many of these problems can be solved, and recognising that team teaching is becoming more acceptable and more enjoyable for many, there are other difficulties on co-teaching which the research by Dahlen in Norway[10] has illuminated. These include the arrangement of the classroom. Where desks are arranged in serried ranks, cooperative work is more difficult than in less formal arrangements where pupils are grouped. Didactic instruction followed by written work also provides more problems than group teaching and project work. By far the most important factor is how the different teaching functions are shared. This can range between the special education teacher being assigned the role of teaching aide and being accepted as an equal partner in planning and carrying out the class programme. On the one hand, the class teacher may plan all activities, carry out all the teaching and simply expect the special education teacher to help individuals with learning difficulties to master tasks set to the class. Alternatively, both teachers may plan the programme, including tasks for children with learning difficulties, share the teaching of the whole class and each give additional help to children who need it. In practice many co-teaching arrangements fall between the two. The future of special educational arrangements of this type will depend on a discussion of these issues and on training to produce the necessary skills for co-teaching.

Withdrawal arrangements

There are always likely to be children who need help individually or in small groups outside the classroom. At best this takes place in a suitably equipped resource room and at worst in any available corner in the school. A major and persistent problem is how to coordinate this work with the children's classroom programme. Too often work in withdrawal groups will be self-contained, assuming that by overcoming learning difficulties in this context, the child will automatically make progress in the ordinary classroom. At the same time the class teacher is left to provide for the children, often without any detailed information about how to plan tasks for them. Communication is left to staffroom comment on progress, more appropriate for discussing emotions than serious educational problems. The best practice, still relatively rare, demands joint planning by the class and special education teachers to see that special help also includes tackling real problems encountered in the classroom while also developing tasks for children to carry out under supervision in the classroom between special sessions. To achieve this degree of collaboration requires an understanding of its importance, a knowledge of materials and above all the feeling of sharing a significant task.

There are other difficulties in developing a resource room withdrawal approach which is flexible and geared to children's special educational needs. One is the set of criteria used to form withdrawal groups. If the procedure is to withdraw all the children with marked problems from one class at a time, their needs may be so dissimilar that a common programme is inappropriate. Less skilled special teachers often offer a single approach hoping it will work with all. Less sympathetic head teachers and teachers with little understanding of learning difficulties often impose withdrawal arrangements which do not allow the special teacher sufficient flexibility. There are obviously organisational and timetable constraints, so that careful thought and imagination is needed in planning cooperative withdrawal arrangements. These need to be based on an adequate assessment of special educational needs, a knowledge of the range of approaches available and a variety of materials and equipment.

Grouping, where necessary, to enhance shared learning should be on the basis of common problems and common needs. Although any individual attention is valuable, much time can be wasted if the short time available is not used effectively by providing a carefully planned individual programme.

Special classes and units in the school

These may be set up by the school or by the local education authority. Classes are most commonly provided for learning and behaviour difficulties but units may be designated for any particular disability or combination of disabilities. In the majority of instances it is very clear that the special class or unit teacher has the principal responsibility for the class programme. The main problems to be tackled are curriculum development and integration.

The curriculum issue has two main aspects, its development from a special education point of view and its relationship to the curriculum of the school. It is typical of the English situation that special class teachers are expected to devise their own curriculum, seldom with any help except from infrequent meetings with colleagues with similar classes. Although techniques and methods may be common, the areas of study may or may not be similar. Compare this approach with that adopted by the mental handicap services in Sweden. Here classes or groups of classes are based in ordinary schools. There is a head teacher responsible for the curriculum and work of classes in a geographical area. Individual teaching strengths are coordinated within a common programme and special education teachers in ordinary schools are supported in the development of their work. Although something similar is evident in some services for the hearing impaired in this country, by and large special classes of all kinds in ordinary schools are too isolated, teachers do not feel part of a team and the quality of education provided depends on individual initiative. A major concern for the future should be the curriculum in special classes.

The second aspect is equally important, although it will vary according to the nature and degree of disabilities catered for and the extent to which the ordinary curriculum needs to be modified. The curriculum in the host school is significant and should influence the special class programme. The closer the relationship possible, the easier it will be for individuals in the special class to join their contemporaries for some activities and, when appropriate, to move into an ordinary class. Secondly, the individual teacher or small group of special educational teachers will not normally have a complete range of expertise in all areas of the curriculum. It enhances the work of special classes if specialists from the host school can contribute to some areas of the curriculum, just as it enhances the credibility and competence of the special class teacher if they teach some things to ordinary classes. Again, much will depend on the climate of personal relationships, the willingness of the special class or unit personnel to be part of the host school and the acceptance by the host school of the special education unit as an integral part of its work.

This leads on to a consideration of the process of integration. As has already been said, the location of a class for children requiring special education in an ordinary school does not necessarily imply that integration will take place. The process has to be positively fostered as research has shown.[8] There needs to be a policy, worked out in the school, which includes both teaching and social situations. Ordinary teachers need to know what to expect and what is expected of them. Special education teachers need to know the school well, know their children, and explore means of supporting them in ordinary classes and around the school. Specific steps may be needed. Peer group tutoring is quite common in the United States as one starting point. For example in a class for very severely disabled children in an elementary school in San Francisco, children in ordinary classes volunteer to spend some time each week, one or two hours, in a one-to-one relationship with the member of the special class, sharing activities, helping their partners and building up relationships. Both partners profit and a basis for ordinary relationships in the school is formed which does not rely solely on incidental contact.

The special class or unit in the ordinary school, even for children with severe disabilities, can provide good quality special education, but above all it can be a starting point for the process of integration. It has the potential to develop good relations between ordinary and special education teachers and between pupils with and without special educational needs. It can become isolated and inward looking and its programme may become unstimulating, but these are problems which need to be tackled. If they can be successfully solved a closer relationship between ordinary and special education will be forged which can only be of benefit to all children in the school.

Particular issues in secondary schools

Special education in secondary schools is more difficult to plan for a number of reasons. In addition to the issues discussed in the previous sections, the larger size of the school and the more complex organisation create their own problems. Perhaps most important of all is the general expectation that success in public examinations is the hall-mark of quality, even when this is obtained by blatant distortions of resource allocations to the more able. Only parents of less successful achievers and children with special educational needs recognise other qualities and they are seldom influential in the community. It is, therefore, difficult for special arrangements to receive sufficient resources, to be given enough priority or to be seen as a useful selling point for schools when they are competing for parental choices.

There are, however, other educational problems relating to the management and organisation of the school and the responsibility of each faculty and subject department. A combination of social and educational objectives normally determines the organisation. The three most common forms of teaching – banding, setting and mixed ability classes – can be found in different combinations. In the first case, the year as a whole is organised into two or three groups based on assumed ability and attainment. In the second pupils are based in forms, which may be banded or based on mixed abilities, and then arranged in sets based on levels of achievement in different subjects. Thirdly, forms will remain mixed in ability. Some schools may have a mixed ability organisation up to the end of the first, second or third year and move to setting gradually over the five-year period. The implications for special educational provision are different in each case.

Where classes are banded, a form which is more common when pupils enter secondary schools at thirteen, the 'bottom' band of lowest achievers is of particular significance. If the variation of the curriculum and the methods used are appropriate, many learning difficulties may not become acute. Special help can be given to the few serious problems on a withdrawal basis, and special education teachers can work closely with subject teachers to develop materials and tasks in 'bottom' band classes for those children with persistent learning difficulties.

Where classes are set, the work of teachers taking sets of the lowest achievers overlaps with special education. Again, withdrawal arrangements may be necessary and joint planning by subject and special education teachers of the work of these sets can limit the need for separate provision.

The mixed ability form of organisation presents the greatest challenge, particularly to the subject teacher. Before considering special educational needs, considerable effort is needed to plan work and develop materials which challenge and extend the ablest, the average and the least successful learner. The special education teacher can help with the latter, develop co-teaching and withdraw some children for additional help.

But there is another major factor which influences all these forms of organisation. This is the extent to which faculties, subject departments and specialist teachers accept responsibility for teaching their subject to all the children in the school including those who have limited literacy skills and those who are slow to learn. Although not expressed so explicitly, there has been a tradition of expecting a level of literacy and competence below which subject teachers do not expect to teach. This was partly due to training, which seldom included provision for the less successful learners, partly due to the status system in the school where high status meant teaching the most able, and partly due to the attitudes of remedial teachers. These attitudes implied that subject teachers did not have sufficient knowledge of learning difficulties and only remedial teachers should be responsible for the curriculum of the slowest learners. There has thus grown up a myth, now being exploded, that children have to be fit for secondary education, and that remedial provision should make them fit or keep them out of the way.

The new approach to special education in the secondary school demands a new relationship between the subject and special education teachers. This can be summarised as follows. Subject departments should be responsible for the teaching of their subject to all children. Their range of expertise is incomplete unless it encompasses not only the ability to teach the able and average, but also the skills necessary to select objectives, materials and methods for teaching their subject to slow learners and semi-literate pupils. The role of the special education teacher is to provide knowledge and experience of the learning difficulties and to use this knowledge to help subject teachers plan their programmes. They should also give special technical help to individuals and small groups who need to develop their learning and behavioural skills. This does not mean that they should not teach ordinary classes and sets as part of their timetable. But it does mean that the responsibility for curriculum objectives and contact should rest on the shoulders of subject teachers. Moves in this direction are being made in many secondary schools, but there is much which still needs to be done to develop this new relationship.

The school special education team

One further point about special education in ordinary schools concerns the importance of developing team work in planning assessment and provision. Each school should have a core team to be joined by peripatetic teachers, educational psychologists, advisers, and health and social service personnel as required. Teams should work at two levels. In primary schools they may be small and rely heavily on outside help. In secondary schools there may be a variety of sub-groups of a transitory or permanent nature to supplement the team.

The two levels in the primary school may be illustrated as follows. At one level the head teacher, deputy and, in big schools, those responsible for year groups, should all meet with a teacher designated to have special education responsibilities, in order to plan the school's overall approach and arrangements. This core team should be supplemented from outside when particular special needs are discussed. The teacher with special education responsibilities may be a class teacher acting as a curriculum consultant or may be an outside teacher with responsibility for special provision in the school. The second level of work would normally involve the head teacher, the special education teacher, the class teacher and, where necessary, outside specialists to consider individual special educational needs.

In secondary schools, team arrangements may be more complex. On the one hand, there is a need to have a significant special education input to senior management decisions. Whatever team is constituted for this purpose it should include a special education coordinator with sufficient experience and status to comment on all aspects of the school's work as it affects special educational provision. At the second level, there will be the need for a group – including house masters or year group teachers, special education teachers and other relevant visiting specialists – to consider individual problems and manage the first three levels of assessment. Finally, other more *ad hoc* groups should be considered, for example, between subject teachers and special education teachers to plan objectives, methods and materials, and between year group teachers and special education teachers to deal with plans for admission, course choices or the preparation for leaving arrangements. There will be many groups set up in secondary schools, but the important new principle is that most, if not all, should be permeated with high quality special education advice.

Special Schools

Institutions for those who are handicapped have existed for over two hundred years. Since the 1944 Education Act the number of special schools has increased threefold. The greatest increase has been in day schools so that in most areas of the country places are available for the majority of those who need them. But despite increasing pressure from advocates of integration, who would like to abolish special schools, they are likely to continue to play an important part in the range of special education available for many years to come. This is partly because primary and secondary schools will continue to set limits on the nature and degree of difficulties for which they can provide, and partly because concentrations of special expertise and experience will continue to be needed to develop special education.

The significant change in recent years has provided a new interpretation to the existence of special schools. The 1944 Education Act implied that the special school was to be the first choice when providing special educational treatment for children ascertained as handicapped. Provision could be made elsewhere, but for most children, falling within the ten categories of handicap defined, the answer was long-term placement in a separate school. The 1981 Education Act, however, abolished categories of handicap and stated explicitly that even where children had severe and long-term disabilities, which required a statement of their special needs, provision should first be sought in the ordinary school. Only if this were not possible should special school placement be considered. This approach is hedged about with conditions, including parental wishes, the use of resources, ability to provide what is needed and the need not to interfere with the education of other children. It is, nevertheless, a major change. Special schools will continue to exist as long as there are limitations in what can be provided in ordinary schools, *but* they will have to justify their existence in terms of what they offer. They are no longer an automatic choice for children assessed to have severe handicaps.

The new legislation implies that special schools must now be more clear about what they offer in terms of curriculum, services and therapies and about their own limits in meeting special educational needs defined in statements. In the previous situation broad unspecified assumptions about the work of special schools were made in the hope that they could meet all the needs of anyone in the categories for which they were designated. The new position, where the statement is a form of contract between the local authority and parents, means that such schools will need to provide defined services.

Before discussing some aspects of the future role of special schools it may be helpful to summarise their current strengths and weaknesses. The most commonly accepted strength is the concentration of knowledge and experience which can be built up by a team working with children with a specific disability or with complex learning difficulties. With good leadership the staff of a special school can share experience and develop a sound know-ledge of the effects of disabilities, and the educational, social and personal difficulties which arise from them. At the same time, the school can develop appropriate variations of the curriculum and methods and materials. The effectiveness of these can be evaluated over a reasonable time-span, particularly in the all-age school. Where the disability requires other therapies it is possible for teachers and therapists to develop cooperative work together. Peripatetic specialists can concentrate some of their efforts. By no means least important, the special school can provide a caring atmosphere in which children receive understanding help in an environment sensitive to their needs.

The major weaknesses are also well known. Schools set up for one category of handicap have not always made a flexible and appropriate response to the wider range and combinations of difficulties now being admitted. A small school for physical and sensory disabilities may have to contend with an ability and achievement range as wide as a comprehensive school ten times its size. A relatively small staff may not be able to provide a sufficiently broad educational programme to meet this range. Concentration on literacy and special methods has often nar-rowed the curriculum. Expectations have not always been high due to isolation from the standards being achieved by contempor-aries in ordinary schools. Children taught with others with the same disabilities over a long period will have few opportunities to interact with other non-disabled children of the same age. The school may provide a shelter which does not prepare them for the life they will have to lead as young adults. In summary, the school may provide an artificial social situation, a restricted range of learning experiences, and few opportunities to experience living and learning among others in the community.

The strengths must not be lost and the weaknesses can be remedied, but to do this requires a major reappraisal of the population of children for whom special schools are needed, a more precise definition of their terms of reference, and much closer association with the ordinary school system than is often the case. It may be relatively easy to decide which children should be the subject of statements and be educated in special schools. But it remains a difficult problem to decide how to group them in relatively small schools, where meeting their educational needs is a practical task.

There are many factors which determine the kind of special schools required. These include the geographical nature of the area to be served and the way in which the population is distributed within it, the differing incidence of disabilities and significant difficulties, and the extent to which primary and secondary schools are able to provide for special educational needs. Whatever the influence of these factors, it remains necessary to reconsider the terms of reference of special schools and the major features which should determine their contribution.

One important feature will be the time an individual is expected to spend in a special school. Because there is now a range of provision, and because individual progress will be reviewed annually to assess the appropriateness of what is offered, more children are likely to move in and out of special schools. Fewer are likely to spend their whole school life in them. It seems likely that four different patterns of attendance should be considered. The first, for a small minority, is the traditional mode, namely, 'full-time long-term' education. This time-scale may be necessary for children with severe complex and multiple disabilities. The second pattern can be described as 'full-time short-term' where a child may attend a special school to acquire special techniques for learning in ordinary schools, perhaps in the case of visual disability, or in the case of children with behaviour difficulties. These patterns exist and are relatively common, but there are also two other patterns emerging. The first can be described as 'part-time' where the child may remain on the register of the ordinary school and attend the special school for a number of sessions each week. This pattern has occurred in some schools for maladjusted children and in some for children with moderate learning difficulties. The final pattern could be described as 'regular short-term intermittent full-time'. This form is not evident in the United Kingdom but has been developed in schools for the visually handicapped in Scandinavia and could become more widespread. In this case children attend their local schools but return each year for short courses in a residential special school which are designed to back up integration with special teaching and experiences. These schools, although having a few children for long-term education, also act as a resource centre for ordinary schools, providing counselling, resources and teacher training.

One of the major implications of the previous discussion is that the chief determinant of the special school's function should be the curriculum it offers. This curriculum should be a variant of that offered in ordinary schools but modified to meet the special educational needs of the children for whom the school is intended. It is no longer appropriate to group children according to their disabilities, when to do so encompasses a very wide range of potential ability, achievement, learning difficulties and personal needs. The range is so wide that in the case of physical and sensory disabilities the small special school is set an impossible task. *Perhaps three examples of curriculum variation may illustrate this approach:

(a)   a curriculum similar in range and level to that taught to the majority in ordinary schools, modified in terms of the special techniques required to teach it and perhaps in terms of the pace at which it is taught. In addition to special techniques, as in the case of visual and hearing disabilities, modifications may include special equipment for the physically disabled and attention to relationships in the case of those with emotional and behaviour problems.

(b)   a curriculum similar in range to that taught in ordinary schools but modified in terms of objectives and pace. Such a curriculum, for children who are slow to learn or who have moderate learning difficulties, should be realistic in terms of what can be accomplished in the time available but have relatively high expectations. It should be much less dependent on literacy skills for access to the normal range of study areas than the ordinary curriculum.

(c)   a curriculum which places major emphasis on the development of social skills and personal autonomy designed for children with severe learning difficulties and degrees of mental retardation. However, the choice of objectives and experiences should reflect those encountered by the majority of children.

It will readily be seen that the first two variants require a close collaboration with ordinary schools and that the second should be closely linked with what is offered to less successful pupils in them. Other variants may be developed but the principle is clear. Special schools should in future offer one and, at the most, two of the variants. It is not an entirely new approach since schools for children with severe learning difficulties (ESN (S) schools in the

---

* Since this section was written the D.E.S has issued guidance distinguishing three similar curriculum variants. 'The Organization and Content of the Curriculum in Special Schools.' D.E.S. Curriculum Note October 1984.

previous nomenclature) have for some years been developing a curriculum which caters for a wide range of disabilities, including physical and sensory ones. Cooperative work has developed between teachers of the blind and deaf and teachers of the mentally handicapped to develop relevant individual programmes within this curriculum framework. All that is suggested is that the principle should be applied to other special schools.

Returning to the four patterns of attendance already described, it can be seen that these will influence the curriculum. Full-time long-term placement will mean that the special school must provide all the educational experiences of the child. The curriculum will need to be broad, covering all common areas of study. Full-time short-term arrangements present the greatest problems since there will be a natural tendency to concentrate on overcoming the child's difficulties. However, unless the curriculum is broad and closely linked to that in the ordinary school, return to an ordinary class may be made more difficult. The third and fourth patterns of attendance present fewer problems. In both cases special schools can rely on the ordinary school to cover the majority of the curriculum and concentrate on special needs and special programmes.

Just as it has proved difficult for small special schools to cover adequately more than one curriculum variant, it will be also difficult for them to offer a variety of patterns of attendance. More information is needed about the special education population but decisions will need to be made to give special schools of the future clear terms of reference and tasks which they are able to accomplish.

The special school as a resource centre

Since the Warnock Committee endorsed this function for special schools, many have embraced it as a means of survival at a time of a falling school population and increased attention to integration. There are a number of pre-conditions to be satisfied before a school can assume this role and in many cases these have yet to be satisfied. First, it should have a well devised and well documented educational programme; secondly it should have a staff with well-developed and confident skills; and thirdly, it should work well with supporting and peripatetic services of all kinds and with health and social service professionals. Out of the quality of its work should come materials and resources which are effective. The staff should be skilled in curriculum development and in devising individual programmes. They should also demonstrate their ability to work collaboratively with others. Finally, the special school should know the constraints under which ordinary schools work and have a good understanding of what goes on in local schools. Thus, there is a necessary period of preparation before special schools assume the functions of a resource centre. Little or inadequate preparation along the lines described may result in the rejection of help by ordinary schools or a steady decline in the use of the special school as a resource centre. The preparation must also include estimating the teacher time necessary for work with ordinary schools and ensuring that it is available without detriment to the school's teaching programme.

What special schools can offer will also depend on the population for which they cater. Every school should have some general skills in assessment and programme planning and each will have special skills which, in the case of schools for moderate learning difficulties and maladjustment, may be more generally useful to primary and secondary schools. Special skills with regard to physical and sensory disabilities will be equally useful in individual cases, but such special schools may have wide catchment areas and be unable to have close and regular contact with ordinary schools.

Of course the kind of resource a special school can offer will depend on how special schools are organised in future, what kind of age-range and time-span they are providing for, and how well they prepare for acting in this way. Special schools can be relatively passive resource centres, on call to other schools, and waiting to be asked for help. They can also be more active with staff working regularly in ordinary schools, receiving pupils for part-time help and providing in-service training for colleagues in ordinary schools. Their functions will be defined by the expectations of the local authority and ordinary schools, by their strengths and by the special educational needs for which they provide. When these are clear and the schools adequately resourced much can be offered. However, these considerations need discussion and are an issue for special education in the immediate future.

Residential special schools

Of all the broad range of provision for special educational needs boarding special schools have the longest tradition. Many of the early schools for physical and sensory disabilities were residential. More recently the provision of schools for children with emotional and behaviour difficulties has included a significant proportion of boarding places. The previous sections have looked at some of the major issues which relate to the educational programme of any special school. It is equally important to examine the reasons for residential placement and look at how they might be influenced in future by changing patterns of child care, particularly in the social services.

One significant feature of the educational system in England and Wales is the prestige accorded to boarding preparatory schools and public schools. In the complex system of social values, attendance at these schools is seen as a means of access to the best in education, to higher status employment and to the establishment. Much as these views have been modified by social changes, boarding schools for ordinary children are considered by many to have a positive value. It is therefore not surprising that many who used them for their own children should consider similar provision for those who are handicapped. These traditional and long-standing views are important in assessing the reasons why boarding special schools form such a large element in the special school field. In Britain the proportion is larger than in many other countries where boarding education in general is less in evidence and has less social significance.

Before the advent of the integration movement some of the grounds for boarding placement were relatively clear cut. First, it was provided for children with disabilities which had a low incidence in the population, such as blindness and deafness, where local provision was not practicable. Secondly, it was recommended for children whose parents could not care for their special needs at home. Thirdly, boarding schools were set up in more sparsely populated areas to provide special education where travelling to day schools was impracticable. Finally, it was seen as creating a therapeutic milieu for children assessed as maladjusted. All these grounds remain valid, but a number of questions now have to be asked.

The relationship between two main areas of work in boarding schools, education and child care, presents the first issue. Whereas major responsibilities for both were originally taken by teachers, two separate professions have emerged. While both teachers and residential care workers may work together in the education programme and in out-of-school hours, it is now more common for residential care workers to be responsible for the quality of living arrangements and out-of-school activities. Both professions lead in their own areas with the assistance of the other. The concentration on domestic-style living and individual care has resulted in a separation of these two areas of work and professional responsibility, so much so that they no longer need be carried out in the same building. More children now live in small units and attend school daily. Although close collaboration is vital between teachers and residential care workers, particularly where children have emotional and behaviour difficulties, the unitary nature of the boarding school run by teachers has been questioned.

Provided that good collaboration exists, it is possible to separate living and learning, with the result that small hostels near day schools are providing an alternative to traditional boarding schools. During the period when this change was taking place in boarding schools, social service departments were, meanwhile, moving away from provision in community homes and placing greater emphasis on special fostering arrangements. These kinds of arrangement can be seen in special education in other countries. In Sweden, for example, the mental handicap service takes houses and flats in residential areas where small groups lead a family pattern of life and attend special schools or classes daily. In Canada at least one provincial school for the physically disabled in Edmonton used to provide foster homes during term time for all who could not attend daily and this system may still exist. A major question for the future is, therefore, where residential care is necessary for social and other reasons, is the boarding school the best answer?

These questions are particularly relevant to arrangements for children with physical and sensory disabilities and mental handicap. The integrated residential community providing both care and education may remain particularly important for children assessed as maladjusted and where behaviour difficulties need skilled management at all times of the day. These difficult needs apart, the case for boarding education is now often a matter of administrative convenience and convention than a coherently argued form of education.

Two other major influences have been evident. The first is the recognition that separation from the family to attend boarding schools is not always helpful to personal development or to the maintenance of family cohesion. The second is the recognition that a distant separation from the home area may inhibit the development of friendship, interests and contacts in a child's neighbourhood, and hence limit subsequent integration in the local community. Integration is a process to which much attention has been given. Better provision in primary and secondary schools has reduced special school admissions, particularly where better local services for the visually and hearing impaired and physically disabled have reduced the need for boarding places. Both the reluctance to place children with disabilities in boarding schools and more specialised provision locally for some of them, have had the effect of calling into question the rationale for residential special education. A major issue for the future is whether it should continue to be provided and if so for whom and in what form.

Peripatetic Services to Ordinary and Special Schools

There are broadly four types of peripatetic services to schools: teaching, advisory, assessment and therapeutic, involving personnel from education, health and social services. Many of the professionals involved have more regular contact with special schools and units than ordinary schools. With every service there are problems of delivery and coordination which are affected by the new legislation and which need to be considered in future planning. These will be discussed first in relation to primary and secondary schools and secondly with respect to special schools.

Advisory and teaching services

The most common form of peripatetic teaching service continues to be the remedial teaching service, usually provided to primary schools but also, in some areas, provided to secondary schools. Although dealing with the child as a whole, detailed work has normally been confined to reading skills. The traditional approach has been for the local service to identify groups of children in individual schools who are considered to have remediable learning difficulties in reading writing and spelling, and to visit the school once or twice weekly to give teaching help to these groups withdrawn from their regular classes. Fundamental changes have taken place and are taking place in the working arrangements and functions of remedial teaching services, but the traditional pattern is likely to persist in some form and a number of limitations should be considered.

A great danger in providing services of this kind is that schools will assume that tackling significant learning difficulties is someone else's responsibility. Class teachers will expect these difficulties to be solved for them as a result of the special teaching provided. They obviously care for the children concerned in their classes but feel relatively incompetent with respect to meeting their needs within the ordinary class programme between special sessions. There are many practical factors which reinforce these attitudes. Remedial teachers may dash in and out of schools, snatching a hasty cup of coffee between sessions and have little time to discuss individual learning difficulties with class teachers. They may seldom if ever see the children working in their ordinary classes and have little time or spare material to provide the class teacher with programmes for the children between sessions. In summary, the activities of the children inside and outside the classroom may be isolated from each other, ill coordinated and the remedial programmes unrelated to the class programme.

The major issue is simply this. While expertise about learning difficulties is limited and not available in all schools, what are the most effective forms of help that can be provided by peripatetic services? Some of the more promising developments are discussed in the following paragraphs on advisory services. There are, however, others which are relevant when the service continues to provide teaching, particularly for children with severe specific learning difficulties. These start from an assessment of the individual's problems which should be wide enough to include classroom behaviour and responses to all aspects of the curriculum. It should include a significant contribution from the class teacher and as a result both teachers should plan a programme which covers work inside the classroom and in withdrawal situations where these are favoured. One of the more promising approaches being adopted is for the visiting teacher to work in the classroom for some periods, giving the children concerned special help, for example with reading and writing, and also with current projects and studies in curriculum areas. At the same time the special education teacher provides the children with appropriate activities for the class teacher to supervise between visits. This last contribution is equally important where children are withdrawn for special help. A further responsibility of the visiting service should be to see that the books and material in the classroom for all activities include appropriate resources for the children with learning difficulties, enabling the class teacher to have available a range of suitable tasks and activities. Time needs to be set aside for planning this form of intervention and the work of visiting special education teachers is a matter requiring considerable attention in the future.

Many remedial teaching services have changed their pattern of activities to include less direct teaching and more advisory work in schools. This builds on the activities discussed in the previous paragraph and concerns helping the class teacher to acquire and develop materials and methods for use with less successful learners and those with special educational needs. But it has gone much further than the joint planning of individual programmes. Members of the service now spend time in the school looking at curricula and class teaching programmes with the school staff to see whether they meet the needs of slower learners and help with learning difficulties. In other words, they look at the whole school response to the pupils who attend it and suggest ways in which it might prevent significant learning difficulties arising. They also look at ways in which special educational needs might be met within the school's own programme, providing assistance and materials to this end. At best this becomes a useful form of in-service training.

This kind of advisory work by teachers concerned with the more common learning difficulties in schools will continue to be most suitable with primary schools. Its development in future may depend on two main factors. The first is that the special education teachers doing advisory work not only have a credible background of primary experience but are also trained to work as advisers with a detailed knowledge of the primary school. The second is that the head teacher and staff of primary schools are aware of special educational needs and their responsibilities to meet them. Above all, they need to work as a team which is receptive to new ideas and which sees professional collaboration with peripatetic services as an essential feature of the school's activities. Local education authority administrators and professional advisers will also need to support these initiatives.

Both primary and secondary schools may also require another form of advisory teaching service related to physical and sensory disabilities. A service of this sort is most commonly available for children with hearing disabilities, is increasing in availability for visual disabilities but is seldom available for children with physical disabilities. The purpose of these services is to see that children with these disabilities, who can profit from being in an ordinary class, receive the technical help and counselling they need from someone experienced in teaching children with their disability. It aims also to provide the class teachers with advice, support, technical equipment and teaching materials. Some services may also provide direct teaching. The advisory teachers may be part of a local education authority peripatetic service or be on the staff of special schools with time allocated to advisory work. The significant feature of this kind of work is the degree of disability it is possible to support in the ordinary class. Although individual children will respond differently to their disabilities, the degree of hearing loss, visual defect or physical disability that can be successfully dealt with in the ordinary class will depend on the effectiveness of collaboration between ordinary teachers and specialist advisory ones. It will depend on providing the former with knowledge, insight into the effects of disabilities on learning, technical equipment and materials. It will depend on joint planning of programmes and also, in many instances, on the specialist teacher having regular sessions with individuals to develop learning skills. If the process of integration is to be actively fostered the work of these advisory teachers will need to be further developed, another item for the agenda when considering the future of special education.

This description of the variety of advisory teachers would be incomplete without reference to perhaps the newest recruits to this field, those providing help with emotional and behaviour difficulties. A start has been made in some areas to provide a service where visiting teachers, experienced in work with maladjusted children, visit schools to give special help with individual problems and hopefully to prevent them becoming so severe that placement in a special school or unit becomes necessary. Such teachers work with individual children and their teachers, providing regular support and counselling. Again they may be on the staff of special schools or part of a peripatetic service. This is perhaps one of the most difficult areas of advisory teaching since behaviour problems have many causes including ineffectual class management as well as problems stemming from the child's relationships, experiences and home circumstances. Head teachers and teachers in the ordinary school may find it much harder to accept that the child has genuine difficulties as compared to their sometimes sentimental acceptance of physical and sensory disabilities. Children may be seen as challenging the authority of teachers and deliberately setting out to make trouble. Some children do, but others are prisoners in a set of unsatisfactory relationships from which they fight to gain release. The work of advisory teachers in this field is also made more difficult by the common 'rotten apple in the barrel' approach which results in schools wishing to see the disturbed child removed and taught elsewhere. Help within the school context is more difficult to accept. There is also an overlap with the work of psychological services which should be recognised. However, this form of advisory teaching is a promising development to which more attention is needed in the future.

A discussion of advisory and teaching services working with

ordinary schools would be incomplete without reference to special education advisers. The presence of experienced special educators in the local education authority's inspection and advisory service is important to the development of special education services which make an effective contribution to primary and secondary schools. Their numbers have been increasing in recent years and few authorities are now without them. The functions expected of them vary and are often combined with general responsibilities for a group of ordinary schools. Their primary duties are, however, to channel the best possible advice on special education to administrators, other advisers and schools about how to meet special educational needs, how to help in the continuing development of special education policy within the authority, and how to develop, maintain and improve the quality of the special education provided wherever it takes place.

To push forward the development of special educational services involves tackling a broad range of problems, many of which have already been discussed. But there are three particular issues on which the future effectiveness of services will depend. Originally the work of many special education advisers was confined to special schools. Some authorities still retain separate advisors for remedial services. If the whole spectrum of special arrangements is to be developed in a coordinated way this separation is no longer appropriate. The special education adviser or advisers in a local education authority need to be responsible for the whole range of services, although a team of more than one adviser would permit specialisation. Secondly, special education advsiers need to work very closely with other general or subject advisers so that no major decisions are taken without special education interests being considered, and so that their work in ordinary schools is supported by their colleagues who are well informed about the approach being adopted towards meeting special educational needs. This involves special education advisers becoming full and active members of the authority's advisory team and not working in isolation.

The final issue, still to be resolved in a number of areas, is the coordination of the work of advisory teaching services. Many of these have been set up on an *ad hoc* basis to meet particular needs. Many work independently so that the service for the hearing impaired has little contact with the remedial service, for example. All the services with trained and/or experienced special educators will be able to provide general advice about special educational needs as well as more specialised help with the kinds of need for which they were set up. Many need welding together in a coherent advisory and support service to schools which would make a more economic use of limited resources. This could mean changes in traditional working practices and moving out of isolated areas of self-interest. This is yet another important item on the agenda for the future of special education.

Advisory assessment services

The work of the advisory teachers obviously includes assessment, but there are other services to schools which take this process further. In the education service, educational psychologists have a major responsibility for helping schools to develop appropriate assessment procedures to identify and provide for special educational needs. At the same time they also bring to bear a more sophisticated battery of assessment techniques on individuals and groups where these are thought necessary to clarify the nature of needs. In the health service doctors, therapists and nurses working with ordinary schools will also play a vital role in diagnosing disabilities and health problems, explaining their implications for a child's education and determining what forms of treatment and therapy might be necessary. When considering the family and social aspects of special educational needs, two other professionals work with schools. From within the education service, the educational social worker, still more commonly known as the education welfare officer, will be a regular visitor with responsibilities for a wide range of contacts with parents. Secondly, social workers from the authority's social service department will also have a contribution to make where children and families fall within their spheres of interest.

All these contributions will be of particular significance at the level or stage (c) of the assessment procedures described earlier. They will involve advice as to how needs might be met in ordinary schools and where more detailed multi-professional assessment may be required. It is not proposed to discuss the work of these important services in detail. The purpose of mentioning them is for completeness and because a continuing issue in special education is the nature and effectiveness of their contribution to schools. Schools will require more detailed information about some children in order to meet their needs but they have to recognise that they need it. They also have to ask more specific questions. It will be a waste of scarce professional time to ask general questions such as 'This child is not learning: why not?' or 'What is the home background?' Much more preparation by the school is necessary. In the first instance,

information needs to be documented about the child's performance, about the skills he has, the tasks he has been set, and the
specific areas of learning and behaviour where difficulties occur.
Descriptions of performance are required. The question can then
be re-posed by saying: 'These are our experiences; these are the
approaches we have made; these are the difficulties we have
experienced. What further assessment is needed and what is your
assessment of the kind of learning difficulties experienced by the
child ?' The bringing together of this sort of information should be
done by the school so that scarce professional time is not wasted
on digging out what the school already knows but has not
presented. Secondly, the school should be in regular contact with
parents so that the home and social situation is known in general
terms and that parents are involved at the earliest stage in
discussing their child's difficulty in school. Of course, these
advisory services will need to help schools develop this information retrieval system by indicating significant data and the means
of obtaining it. If, however, they are to improve their contribution
in future, schools will have to improve the ways in which they
gather and communicate information about a child's performance. This concerns their general assessment and recording
system for all children as well as those additional elements
devised to identify and assess special educational needs.

Peripatetic education services to special schools

The work of special schools can be enhanced by visiting teachers,
advisers and psychologists in a different way from ordinary
schools. The staff are likely to know about learning difficulties and
will not require the learning difficulty or behaviour difficulty
teaching service. However, teachers with experience of physical
and sensory difficulties are not always available as members of staff
of schools for moderate and severe degrees of mental handicap,
and such schools may need the help of peripatetic services for
those disabilities. Because the population in special schools is
becoming, and will continue to become, more mixed in respect of
the combinations of disabilities and difficulties, and because the
curriculum offered may become a major criterion for admission,
there will be a greater demand for collaborative work to understand needs and plan individual programmes. This is being
recognised in schools for severe degrees of mental handicap
where this is commonly combined with visual, hearing and
physical disabilities. It is equally necessary in schools for those
with moderate degrees of mental retardation which are also often

combined with other disabilities. One effect of a long period of thinking in categories, is to continue to assume that most children fall neatly into them and that teachers with training and experience with those categories can cater for all their needs. This has resulted in the isolation of different specialist teaching teams with hierarchies of prestige. Only comparatively recently has the broad common basis of all special educational needs been recognised together with the realisation that different specialist teachers should work more closely together. The future work of special schools will require a much greater collaboration with visiting specialist teachers.

One more area requiring further attention is the curriculum of special schools. It has not been common for advisers and advisory teachers with responsibilities for subjects and areas of study to work regularly with special schools. This is partly because they have seen special education as a separate area to which they have little to contribute. Comparative ignorance of the needs of the children concerned has reinforced this view. It is also partly due to the fact that special schools have exaggerated their 'specialness' and the differences of their children and have not always recognised the need for an input from subject advisers. Although this situation is changing, the quality of the curriculum in special schools will in future depend on an increased understanding and use of the best curricula, methods and materials from ordinary schools.

Continuity

Many educational systems, and those in England and Wales are no exception, place great emphasis on the work of individual schools and plan primary, secondary and special school provision separately. Children move from infant to junior and junior to secondary schools at set chronological ages. Moving from one school to another is a major event in a child's life. For many it occurs smoothly because the individual adjusts easily and the schools concerned have a knowledge of each other's work and have planned arrangements which are sensitive to the common problems and anxieties of the children moving from one school to another. For other children it may be a traumatic event, ill prepared for and crudely dealt with. For children with special educational needs, transfer arrangements and continuity in the help they receive are of especial significance.

The problems which may arise are often made worse by two features which are common to nearly all moves from class to class or from school to school. The first might be termed the 'fresh start philosophy'. Records, more often concerned with behaviour and attitudes to work than with programmes taught, skills mastered and ideas understood, are often seen as 'crime sheets'. The situation in the new class or school is different, and the child needs to be given a 'clean' start uninfluenced by his or his previous teachers' experiences to date. This is closely linked with the second feature, the individual teacher's reluctance to accept the opinions of colleagues in other schools or classes. The wish to make up their own minds about children in their classes. It is still common to hear teachers saying, 'I like to make up my own mind. I don't look at records for the first month or two until I have got to know my class.' If this approach is applied throughout a child's school career from five to sixteen years of age, some ten to twenty months out of a total of perhaps ninety in the ten-year period may be wasted in rediscovering individual needs and not providing a continuity of approach to them. Of course it is easy to understand this essentially charitable attitude to records when they are only concerned with judgments of behaviour and do not contain useful information about performance, materials and approaches used which might be built on. Changes are occurring, but for the child with special educational needs it is vital to develop a smooth means of passing information between teachers and schools which enable special help to be continued without a break and without reassessment at each phase.

Continuity in approach to individuals should be matched by some continuity in the forms of provision in different phases of education. Again it is still relatively common to consider arrangements in primary schools separately from arrangements in secondary schools and not to consider the overall pattern of such arrangements throughout the compulsory school period. Moreover, in the case of special educational needs it is still assumed that they are short-term and remediable, although a number may be long-term and persistent, such as severe specific learning difficulties, mild and moderate degrees of mental handicap, and the less severe forms of physical, sensory, speech and language disabilities. The need for developing services and arrangements in schools which provide a continuity in care, concern and special education throughout the whole school life of the individual is thus of prime importance.

CHAPTER 7

Major Issues Shared with Others

Special education cannot be provided effectively in isolation. Although it is the responsibility of education services in many, if not all, developed countries, many other professions also make vital contributions to its provision. This chapter looks at a number of important issues which arise in multi-professional patterns of work during the compulsory school period and even more significantly in the pre-school period and the period of transition from school to adult life. It also considers the changed status of those who are handicapped and their parents as they have moved from an almost total dependence on professionals to at best a shared partnership in planning to meet their needs.

Relationships between Professions

Many of the current issues cannot be fully understood without looking at the changes in responsibility and in the territories in which they are exercised. Current problems often have their roots in previous struggles to gain recognition and to avoid relinquishing administrative control. This is most clearly seen in the health services. At the present time, in France and a number of other countries, the Ministry of Health is responsible for the institutions in which the one or two per cent of those most severely handicapped are cared for, trained and educated. The Ministry of Education supplies teachers to work in these institutions, but doctors and, in most cases, psychiatrists, determine and manage their regimes with the help of nurses, therapists, teachers and other personnel. In other countries the reverse is the case, with the Ministry of Education providing the schools, and health services giving medical and therapeutic help within them. Within the health services changes have also taken place. For example, in the United Kingdom nursing has become a separate service working with doctors but with an independent status responsible for managing nursing care within a framework of medical recommendations. The same is true of therapeutic professions where physiotherapy and special therapy services are independently managed in a similar way. It has been a major upheaval within the health service for doctors to have given up absolute control and to collaborate in the planning of treatment regimes. The best ways of planning a coordinated delivery of all the various elements are still not fully accepted by all concerned.

The difficulties which arise are most evident when meeting the special educational needs of children in institutions run by other services. In the pre-school period playgroups and day nurseries are the responsibility of social services. During the school period provision in hospitals and community homes gives rise to problems. In the post-16 education, employment, health and social services may all make different arrangements for those who are handicapped. Special education personnel, therefore, have to fit into different patterns of teamwork developed by other services as well as developing a team approach with other professionals within the education service. Those concerned in the education service need to be well-informed about the duties, procedures and institutions of other professionals and vice versa. Often information about the different patterns of working, legal responsibilities and services of other professionals is scanty and not well presented so that myths persist and misunderstandings arise.

Perhaps two positive principles are emerging which encourage better working arrangements. First, it is now recognised that professionals in one service work in provision made by other services, so that teachers work in hospitals and community homes, social workers in schools and hospitals and health service personnel in community homes and schools. This means that professional territories are no longer confined to institutions in their own service. One continuing difficulty which becomes more marked in times of limited resources is that undue priority may be given to one's own service and institution so that, for example, health services given to other institutions, such as schools, may be insufficient.

The second principle is less clearly established but is equally important to team working. This is that the advice offered by different professionals should be primarily concerned with their own field. The provision of special education and the designation of where it takes place is an educational decision and, similarly, the provision of medical and nursing care or social casework and childcare is the responsibility of health and social services. The temptation to recommend that other services provide alternatives is particularly great when resources are limited. Teams, however, work better when each profession only offers the services and makes the recommendations which can be implemented by that service.

The coordination of teamwork in case conferences and special educational programmes is also an area of difficulty. Again a useful principle is becoming established that the coordination of a meeting is the responsibility of the professionals in whose office or institution it is taking place. This coordination will also be influenced by the service taking the major responsibility during a phase in the child's life. The next sections consider the major phase.

The Pre-School Years

More obvious disabilities will be evident at or soon after birth and it will be at this stage that health services will intervene. Midwives, health visitors, general practitioners and hospital maternity units will often be the first professionals to be aware of the disability. The first need is, in almost all instances, support, counselling and guidance for the parents. This is a process which needs to take place over time to help achieve a positive acceptance of the baby and to give information about how he or she may be helped in the early years. Paediatric assessment may be arranged in the early days and child-care arrangements suggested to the parents. Parents' groups may also provide very real support at this stage by sharing experiences of having a child who is disabled or very retarded. They help to bring the parents into a network of caring relationships. The 1981 Education Act also encourages consultants to put parents in touch with voluntary organisations. for particular disabilities where appropriate.

At this point, education services have two main functions, to ensure that health services know of their pattern of special education provision, so that parents can be given this information, and to be ready to provide pre-school help when it is needed and requested by parents. The first of these functions is facilitated where educational psychologists and specialist teachers are regular members of development assessment teams, although their contribution may be limited in the early months.

Many children will not immediately be seen to have disabilities or developmental delays and this is where primary healthcare teams need to remain alert during the first two years of a child's life. One of the most positive of recent developments is the introduction of screening programmes carried out by community nurses to pick up early indications of potential difficulties which might need further investigation at child assessment or paediatric clinics. Again, good contact between education services and pre-school health services and clinics can ensure an early warning of special educational needs and for some children the provision of home-visiting teaching services.

Early intervention at the critical stages of development is vital if the handicapping effects of disabilities are to be minimised. Programmes which parents can manage are essential because it is not usually possible to provide regular professionals help to all families. It is the management of these programmes which causes some tension between professions. There needs to be a psychological and educational input to their development, supervision and evaluation but their day-to-day management can be undertaken by many responsible adults with training and supervision. The question arises of which adults in which professions. It is essential to set up a small interdisciplinary team from all relevant professions to supervise this form of intervention and to allocate available resources. This will prevent the continuation of an *ad hoc* approach which may depend on which profession the parents have most contact.

A second major area in which concerns are shared is in the provision for young children with disabilities and developmental difficulties in playgroups, day nurseries and nursery schools. Playgroups, supervised by local authority social services, and day nurseries run by them, may accept children known to be handicapped and also discover disabilities after admission. In both instances the question arises as to what form of special help is needed or available. To some extent this depends on the programme of activities, and on how far care or training predominates. A relatively passive approach to the needs of all the children will not necessarily result in a wish to provide actively for those with disabilities; difficult behaviour may be the main stimulus for seeking help. A lack of response to a more active programme on the other hand will be more likely to result in help being sought. Assessment services may be consulted including those provided by the school psychological service. Under the 1980 Education Act it is now possible to provide for teachers to work in day nurseries where desirable. Education and social services can cooperate by offering to those pre-school groups specialist peripatetic teaching services to advise on the programmes for children with disabilities and to ensure that playgroups and day nurseries know who to contact when they need help.

It is during the pre-school years that the relative contributions of teachers and social workers may first need clarification. The latter will have the training and resources to help families with the care of their children when family and social difficulties are referred to them. They may not have the information necessary and experience with disabilities to help families when the care of a disabled child is causing problems. Similarly, teachers working with parents of children who are handicapped may come across family problems and situations with which they are not trained to deal. Both professions need to know the work of the other, and better means of collaboration must be found if parents are to get the services they need and not suffer from too many people trying to help them, or no one understanding their needs.

A final feature of the pre-school years is the setting up of special nurseries or nursery classes in special schools for children with severe disabilities. Many are seen as important situations in which the special education needs of children with very complex learning difficulties are assessed over a period of time as they respond to planned individual programmes. In this setting co-operation between different services is an essential ingredient of adequate assessment and appropriate programmes. The HMI Survey of education for 'Young Children with Special Educational Needs'[10] stated that 'in the nurseries where assessment was multi-disciplinary and where professionals, in addition to nursery teachers and nursery nurses, shared in the process of individual programme planning, education was of a better quality ... Some of the most valued support to nurseries, whether special or ordinary, was said to come from child assessment units in their localities. Nurseries from three authorities referred to the high degree of co-operation and the quality of information from these sources.'

The pre-school years are an important phase in the growth and development of all children and particularly vital for children with disabilities and significant difficulties. During these years all three major services have a part to play, together with voluntary organisations and parents' groups. Early detection, diagnosis and assessment of special educational needs requires planned cooperation by health, social and education services and collaboration between the professionals who work in them. A start has been made but much remains to be done if the best use is to be made of available resources and if the work of different professionals is to be coordinated in the best interests of the child and the family.

The School Years

Many of the aspects of the work of visiting teachers and advisers discussed in the previous chapter as needing development apply equally to the work of other visiting professionals from health and social services. In particular, these concern the sharing of information, assessment and co-operative patterns of work in ordinary and special schools.

Information

Where disabilities and significant difficulties have been discovered in the pre-school years it is obviously very helpful if schools know of them before the children concerned enter infant schools. Other special educational needs may only emerge as children respond to the school programme and learning difficulties of all kinds are revealed. Turning to the first of these groups, doctors, nurses and therapists in the health service and social workers may be aware of children with disabilities and have worked with them and their parents. Some may also have been seen regularly by home visiting teachers. It is very important that these children's difficulties be understood by the staff of the schools they enter, but the passing of relevant information about them is often made difficult by a number of factors. First, the staff of the ordinary schools may have little knowledge of special educational needs and the conditions that give rise to them. Busy professionals in other services with limited time may not be able to devote time to the in-service training needed. They may, therefore, not give information because they fear it might be misunderstood, misused, and not to the advantage of the child's education. Secondly, the health and social service professionals may not realise the significance of their information for planning the child's educational progress in school. The effects of the disabilities and difficulties on learning may not be fully appreciated. Thirdly, and perhaps most important, the information may only be made available in terms of their own professional language and discipline. An accurate medical diagnosis may mean little to teachers and a social assessment of family situations may mean little in education terms without interpretation. It is necessary for these professionals in other services to learn to interpret their information and present it to schools in terms of its educational implications. If necessary they will need to consult with special educators to develop more awareness of the potential learning difficulties which may arise from the conditions they describe.

Confidentiality

The sharing of information cannot be discussed without the question of confidentiality arising. Parents give professionals information for their ears alone. The professional–client relationship is seen in many instances to preclude the passing on of some information given during consultations or during therapeutic and counselling situations. This allied to the fact, already noted, that professionals do not consider other professionals, in this case teachers, able to understand their fields provides a barrier to communication. A real barrier of confidentiality is thus reinforced by professional barriers which guard expertise.

There are many solutions to the problem of confidentiality, but before turning to them it is worth considering what information should be confidential. Professionals need to know what should be confidential and what should not, helping their clients to recognise this distinction. Thus a complete medical report cannot be confidential if the child has a disability which is obvious to all. Secondly, other professionals may not need to know the cause of the disability or difficulty if this is confidential information. They only need to know its effects on their work. A much clearer picture of the criteria for keeping information private to the professional and client is required so that open communication is encouraged and only that information which is detrimental to or unnecessary for the education of the child kept under wraps.

The problems surrounding confidentiality can be reduced if a number of other factors are recognised. First, parents have control over the information available to them. In practice, when they establish confidence in other professionals such as teachers, the parents themselves pass on this information. Secondly, reports for schools and the education service can be confined to the implications of clinical conditions and family circumstances for care and education, always remembering that schools will need to work particularly closely with the parents of children with special education needs. Finally, and probably most important, is the question of the need for other professionals to take necessary actions that are not in the control of the professional with confidential information. This means that those with confidential information, which needs to be known by other services if they are to take appropriate actions, must make it clear to parents and clients that what they can do may be limited unless they can indicate to others a sound basis for making particular arrangements. It may take time and counselling to persuade parents of the necessity of passing on information. It also requires an active desire on the part of the professional to share what is necessary in the client's best interests. What is important is that the worker first given the confidential information should recognise when this should be shared if others are to cooperate in meeting a child's needs.

Working in isolation from one another creates professional barriers to communication, while regular contact encourages trust and sharing when personal relationships are good. Accepting parents as partners in assessment and decision-making also results in more open communication. Professionals with intermittent 'hit and run' contacts with children with special educational needs still need to recognise the contribution of those with the longest periods of contact with the children, namely parents, teachers and care workers. If these three important influences in children's lives are to work effectively to mitigate the effects of disabilities and difficulties they need to be well informed.

Assessment

Health and social service professionals will assess children in their own clinics and centres and also work in schools, helping with assessment at the third level or stage outlined in chapter 6. In the case of the former the process will not be primarily directed to special educational needs: the problem is to ensure that the child's education is an element in the assessment and that there is sufficient knowledge of what goes on in a range of schools to include this element. An educational input by teachers or educational psychologists in the assessment team and full reports from the child's teachers are means of achieving this. There are other problems, for example, if medical treatments are prescribed and the effects on the child's learning performance not communicated to his teachers. Decisions may be taken by social services to place children with adoptive parents, foster parents and in community homes without seeing whether local ordinary or special schools can meet their educational needs. These assessments outside the school may also include attendance at child guidance and child psychiatric clinics. It is all too easy for schools to be characterised as unhelpful or uncooperative. It is easy to make assumptions about school because everyone has attended one. It is much more difficult to cooperate with teachers to get a realistic appraisal of the child's current school situation and the possibilities which exist within it for meeting any special needs. This is an area of work requiring time, regular interaction and joint planning which continues to need sustained attention in the development of special education services.

Where professionals from other services contribute to assessment in schools many of these difficulties need not arise. Familiarity with the school will result in appropriate weight being given to teacher opinion and a realistic appraisal made of what is possible. The main problem is whether these professionals are consulted at an early enough stage of the child's learning difficulties. Pressures in the school, previous experience and the work-load of the visiting specialists may result in their being consulted only when the school is at the end of its tether. By that time all the staff want is for the child to be placed elsewhere. When this is not possible and solutions must continue to be sought within the school, visiting professionals can get a reputation of being unhelpful. There remains much to be done to inform schools of the limits of the work of other services, of the kinds of problem for which help can be given and the importance of early referral for consultation before the child's difficulties become too acute.

Cooperative patterns of work

As with visiting teachers the work of therapists, particularly in the fields of speech and physiotherapy, is enhanced where the therapist and the teacher work together. This is often easier in special schools where therapists have regular sessions than in an ordinary school where children may attend health clinics for treatment. Cooperation is often at its best when therapists work in the classroom and teachers and aides can see what is done and carry on practice programmes in the therapist's absence. It is at its worst when the therapist and the teacher never meet, and treatment and education are seen as two separate, unrelated activities. The field of speech and language disorders is a good example of a special educational need where changes may be required. These problems, common with younger children, are at present the primary responsibility of speech therapists in the health service who are under pressure to provide hospital-based services and have less time available for work with ordinary and special schools. At the same time there are very few special education teachers with specific training in this field. The position is very different in other countries. In Norway, for example, the teaching of children with speech and language disorders is one of the specialisations within special education teacher training. The bulk of the work with children with these special needs in schools is carried out by these teachers. Speech therapists within the health service can then concentrate on the smaller number of complex difficulties experienced by children and adults. Cooperative patterns of work may also require some reallocation of responsibilities in the future.

Most of the points discussed in connection with the school years apply equally to professionals working in ordinary and special schools. However, special schools normally know more about the work of visiting specialists while the latter are often more knowledgeable about special schools than ordinary schools. The best sharing of information and cooperative working can be seen in special schools. In future, as more provision of all kinds is made for special educational needs in primary and secondary schools it will be important for these good practices to be adopted.

The Post-Compulsory School Years: Transition

Going to a school, whether ordinary or special, represents a normal pattern of life for parents of children who are handicapped. Although they may have many extra day-to-day problems of care, they are now helped, like all other parents, by a recognisable education programme for their children over the compulsory school period. Parental concerns are now more sharply focused on the kind of adult life their children will lead, particularly after they are no longer able to help them, and on the education, training and support services which will help their children make the transition from school to adult life. This is a priority for action in all the member countries of OECD and accounts for their strong support for the OECD/CERI Transition project funded by the United States and member countries, and which is being carried out at the time of writing. The project has been seeking to clarify the major issues, identify and describe innovative practices and disseminate information. The OECD/CERI project distinguished three phases in transition: the final school years; vocational and social training, and continuing education after them; and the early years of adult and working life. Although special education services may only be concerned with the first two of these phases, a knowledge of the whole field of transition is vital.

The aims of transitional arrangements are an important starting point. Traditionally, the end of the compulsory school period was followed by a return to parental care or long-term placement in an institution. For those young people at home some day centre and training centre provision was made. The most able and academically successful might, with difficulty, obtain employment often well below the level of which they were capable. Some traditional vocational and craft skills might be taught to others to be used in sheltered workshops. Expectations for young people considered handicapped were relatively low both in respect of employment potential. These expectations on the part of those educating and training the young people were reinforced by uninformed public attitudes and a generally charitable but undemanding approach.

However, recent decades have seen considerable changes. Opportunities to develop social and life skills have increased and more provision is being made for adults who are handicapped to live independently in special housing and small personalised homes in the community. A wider range of employment skills are being included in programmes and a broader spectrum of employment is being developed. Even in a time of high youth unemployment, small advances are being made. The aims of transition are becoming clearer and policies in many countries are reflecting them. These aims now include preparation for living in the local community as independently as possible, for working in open or sheltered conditions as far as possible in association with others, and for having opportunities for recreational and leisure activities with others within the same facilities. Of course progress has not been fast enough, training programmes need further development and dissemination, new opportunities for useful work need to be explored and more semi-independent living arrangements need to be available. Education, social and employment services have to change their patterns of work and support and define practicable objectives towards these aims. All too often programmes and arrangements are made to solve immediate problems without looking ahead. For example, pupils who are mentally handicapped may be retained in special schools over the age of sixteen simply because no other possibility exists and not because education between sixteen and nineteen is part of preparation within an overall transition programme.

The period of transition may be assumed to cover the period from about fourteen years of age to the early twenties, but the age range over which education and training is offered may be much shorter. Some countries, including the USA and Sweden, have most young people with disabilities and significant difficulties in the education system up to twenty-one years of age. In England and Wales parents still have to fight to get education for their children after the age of sixteen. The first major point about transition is to gain more widespread recognition that all children and young people classed as handicapped can benefit from extended education and training programmes. They need them if they are to lead a more independent, satisfying and useful existence and are not to remain over-dependent on others throughout their lives. There is already evidence to show that living in the community with support services is less costly in financial terms, even for many with severe disabilities. Therefore resources devoted to effective transitional programmes are likely to reduce the long-term burden of institutional care. But the main argument should not be financial, it should be based on the quality of life which any society offers to its handicapped members. Quality, although hard to define, is where individuals have a choice and a normal rhythm of daily life in much the same circumstances as their non-handicapped contemporaries.

It is during the transitional phase that the situation-specific concept of handicap discussed in chapter 2 becomes particularly vital. Young people's disabilities and significant difficulties will be considered handicapping in different ways. In the education service any individual receiving special education may be broadly defined as educationally handicapped. On leaving school each of the other three major services will adopt their own sentence for determining who they consider handicapped. Social services will look at the need for family support and the capacity to live independently; employment services will carry out an analysis of job skills; and industrial safety and health services will assess the need for continued treatment and therapy. One or two examples illustrate the changing nature of handicap. A young person who is blind and who has received effective special educational support may achieve high academic levels in school and college. But when that individual seeks employment different criteria may be applied, opportunities may be more limited and the handicapping effects greater. On the other hand an individual with a moderate learning difficulty may be very handicapped in school, but, given good preparation, he may not be handicapped in gaining and retaining employment when it is available. The employment services will not consider him handicapped. Thus, when leaving school, whether or not an individual is categorised as handicapped will depend on the criteria used by different services and agencies, and it is necessary for those in special education to know what these criteria are. Preparation for transition involves recognising the changing concept of handicap in this phase and teachers responsible for leavers should work closely with other professions in order to understand their frames of reference.

The final school years

There is a sense in which the whole school curriculum prepares the individual for adult life from the earliest years. The traditional academic curriculum, however, often leaves out social and life skills and relies on families to cultivate them. Aspects of preparation for leaving school have entered into the programme of less academic pupils, but it has been in special schools where most thought has been given to developing leaving courses. For these who are handicapped it is particularly important that they leave school well prepared for the next stage in their life. Those integrated into secondary schools have often had less preparation of this kind. So courses should be reviewed to take account of changing social patterns and employment prospects. This demands that teachers are well informed about prospects for further education, vocational and social training, employment and living conditions. They need to know the criteria used by other institutions and agencies for admission to courses and the range of services available to those who are handicapped after leaving school. It is necessary to see the final years of schooling as the beginning of the transition process and not as an end to education.

Although the progress of children receiving special education should be reviewed annually, there is a special need for a complete reassessment at the beginning of the final year or two of schooling. This reassessment should not only include health, educational and social service personnel but also those who know the employment situation. It is now common for careers teachers and careers officers to be involved. But attention to further training and employment is not sufficient even for those where jobs are available. Attention to the social life the young people are likely to lead and the skills necessary for active participation in community activities is equally important as part of this assessment. This process of reassessment is one where professionals from different services and agencies can begin to cooperate in planning transitional arrangements. To do this requires information about available choices. It is still common for parents to complain that they have little information and for professionals not to know what each other's services are offering.

The reassessment process should also involve looking at how well the young people and their parents are adjusted to the disabilities concerned and how they view future prospects. These are aspects where counselling is often essential. The period of adolescence is often one of difficult readjustment for all young people and their parents. It can be even more difficult for young people who are handicapped. Not only do they become increasingly aware of the effects that their disabilities might have on their career aspirations, their personal relationships and their life style, but they also have to cope with these problems when their parents are uncertain of the way ahead. The parents are more uncertain than other parents of teenagers since they are seldom well informed about prospects for their children and are often more acutely aware of the difficult balance between continued protection and risk-taking. It is perhaps less important which service should provide the necessary counselling than that young people and their parents should have ready access to someone with counselling skills.

There are two aspects of this counselling process which are as yet not sufficiently well developed. The first relates to the expectations of the young people. Although realism about future prospects is important, aspirations are often set too low for the more severely disabled. They still have to struggle against even the professionals' expectations to have more and better opportunities. They are often railroaded into conventional low-level courses and occupations. This counselling needs to be more imaginative. The other aspect is that parents are seldom included in long-term counselling processes. Many parents will say that special education is good at involving them in pre-school programmes but it offers little or nothing to the parents of adolescents who are handicapped. They get no help in dealing with their children's difficulties in growing up or in preparing them for adult life. One interesting example is provided by a folk high school in Copenhagen for young adults who are mentally retarded. It has developed effective courses in communication, social and leisure skills, together with continued general education. Early on, parents' groups were formed to discuss their children's progress. It was found that sustained counselling was necessary before parents were able to accept the exercise of new skills such as independent travel, self help etc. The early stages, the school's work was inhibited by parents' fears, anxieties and limited understanding of practical possibilities. Thus counselling for young people and their parents is important if their full potential is to be realised and transition programmes are to be effective.

Training and continuing education

It is during this second phase of the transition process that most difficulties arise, either because of a lack of appropriate provision or because of the gaps and overlaps between different fields of responsibility. Discontinuities emerge and there is a general lack of planning and coordination. The major options may be tabulated as follows:

(a)   Continuing in school over sixteen years of age for three reasons:
  (i)   to continue with academic studies for access to higher education;
  (ii) to prolong a necessary education programme for young people with severe degrees of physical, sensory and mental disabilities before entering employment or vocational training in day centres;
  (iii) because there is no other provision and parents wish for continued education between sixteen and nineteen years of age.

(b)   Entering an ordinary college of further education for one of the following reasons:
  (i)   to follow a general education course for public examinations;
  (ii) to follow a normal college course for preparation for a technical or vocational skill area;
  (iii) to follow a bridging course to prepare for access to (ii);
  (iv) to follow a special course for students who are handicapped which aims at further general vocational preparation;
  (v)   to follow a special course for the continued general education of students who are handicapped;
  (vi) to follow a course within the range of those finance and set up in collaboration with the manpower services commission.

(c)   Entering a special college for the further education and vocational training of students who are handicapped.

(d) Entering courses provided by the employment services in vocational training centres and rehabilitation centres.
(e) Entering open employment.
(f) Entering sheltered employment.
(g) Attending an adult training centre or day centre.
(h) No post school provision.

Not all the options exist in all areas and each area will need to make its own map of possibilities and gaps. There are more examples of this being done by local authorities than there were but there are still not enough.

The first major difficulty is getting agreed criteria for each option. The second is that the options (a) to (e) only cover as yet a small percentage of the 16+ age group who are handicapped. A third is that options(g) and (h) are in many respects the easiest to provide and that considerable efforts have to be expended to ensure that the others are available. Finally, options (d), (e), (f) and (g) may or may not be available after options (a), (b) and (c) have been exercised. This makes programmes difficult where the age of entry may range from 16+ to 19+ with different levels of achievement and skill.

The array of possibilities in England and Wales is a common array in many countries but different elements are given different weight. The common factor is that young people with disabilities usually have to be more proficient for their level of general ability than their non-disabled contemporaries to gain entry to many courses. The effect of this is to push the disabled group further down the scale of provision than the distribution of their potential would warrant, so that too many young people end up in low level employment, sheltered workshops and day centres just because they are disabled.

There is, however, one outstanding issue in this second phase of transition and this is the question of vocational preparation and employment. The starting point is that young people with disabilities have a right to be considered for employment; however difficult the labour market they should have a reasonable share of the available opportunities. They should not be excluded simply on account of a particular difficulty. Expectations need to be reasonably high. For example, many young people who are mentally handicapped are capable, with effective training, of open employment. Thus in the USA mentally retarded girls, who in other countries might go from school to day centres, are able to carry out laboratory testing techniques in an oil company laboratory. Although this is a demonstration project it shows what can be done. The training technology now exists to raise the level of performance of many with severe handicaps to that acceptable to employers. Vocational training is important particularly where it is carried out in real situations. On the other hand, there is increasing evidence that training to master the skills necessary for a particular job is relatively easy. What is often more difficult is to master an adequate array of social and life skills needed to maintain employment. Making relationships, functioning effectively in social situations and being able to be as autonomous as possible as an individual are crucial. These skills are even more important when employment is not available.

The main problem is that most emphasis is still placed on vocational skills. Governments allot resources for a skilled labour force, so that courses in colleges and vocational training centres have to concentrate on preparation for particular jobs. The Staff involved are chosen because of their technical proficiency as skilled workers and results are judged by vocational proficiency and job placements. The position is changing. Special schools have long realised the need for social and life skills in their courses for leavers and the Further Education Unit has recognised their importance in many useful publications on the curriculum.[12] But still major responsibilities and resources are given to Manpower Services to produce a skilled work force and the more general areas of personal development and social adjustment, while recognised, are subordinated to providing for different sectors of industry and commerce. Employability is a major criterion for acceptance in courses and this is defined primarily in terms of job skills. Courses are relatively short, allowing little time in many instances for social and life skill development. Often the staff involved are not trained and experienced in this area. This is not simply an issue in the United Kingdom, it is common in many developed countries including the USA.

Even when open employment is not considered a realistic objective, work skill development often dominates the programme in sheltered workshops and adult training centres of all kinds. Programmes in these centres are often inward looking and carried out in isolation from any preparation for independent living because the agency responsible for the centre training is not responsible for developing independent living skills or because different staff in the agency are responsible.

There are two main points which need continued attention. First, that useful work is an essential aspect of adult status in the community. Young people categorised as handicapped should be enabled to perform useful work like any other citizen. If open employment is not possible what alternatives are available? This is an issue which has not been tackled for fear of weakening the case for the employment of the disabled. Now that youth unemployment is more widespread and likely to remain a feature of modern societies it will be necessary to explore alternatives for all young people including those who are handicapped.

The second point is how to develop a better balance between vocational and social training during the transition period. This may be easier to achieve in special schools and in special colleges than in ordinary colleges and work preparation centres. Some agencies in the United States provide both sheltered workshops and small residential units in which self care skills, independent living and recreational skills are taught alongside work skills in an integrated programme. The same is true of a number of the arrangements made by the New Zealand Society for the Mentally Handicapped. There are other examples, but on the whole most of these centres tend to specialise in either vocational training or social training. An integrated approach through cooperation between different professionals in education, social and employment services to look at the balance of transitional programmes is a major issue for the future.

The question of gaining real experience has long been recognised in arrangements for young people to spend periods in different offices, businesses and factories and to look after themselves in camps, on expeditions and during periods in residential settings. More recently this has been the subject of discussion in terms of the merits of on-site and off-site training. Three work experience centres in Australia illustrate the differences in approach. These centres provide vocational training for school leavers considered handicapped over a period of up to a year and then support individuals in the early months of employment where this is obtained. The one centre in the Sydney area pioneered an approach based on workshops and teaching areas in the centre where a variety of light engineering and other skills are taught. An educational and social programme runs alongside this, tailing off rowards the end of the course when full-time working is expected. The centre is a hive of interesting activity. The other two centres in Adelaide and Brisbane are relatively empty. Work is sought in local factories and in the community, and groups of students work with their instructors in enclaves or on community projects. Only social training and continued education is carried out in the centres. Teacher/counsellors and instructors work together in planning programmes but work preparation is off site and involves real experience. A similar approach to living skills is adopted by the Queensland Health Authority Service for the mentally handicapped. Houses are leased in the community, groups of five or six young people are moved in with staff, and start living. As training programmes develop staff supervision is reduced and withdrawn. The argument is that staff training young people in a centre or institution can only simulate situations and seldom consider their charges ready for the independence of which they are capable. The scheme of off-site training is effective, challenging and when successful the group can be left to live on their own with minimum supervision. This question of on-site and off-site training is also debated in the USA. Off-site training appears to have many advantages and could with profit be considered in this country. It does involve professions working away from the territories in which they may feel secure, and professional barriers to this approach may have to be overcome. It could, however, solve a number of problems. For example, Adult Training Centres need never be full in the sense of having places for everyone in the centre every day. With proper staffing many students could be living and working out in the community.

The second phase of transition, continued education and training after the compulsory school period, is a vital one for young people who are handicapped. Most need extended training and experience if they are to minimise the handicapping effects of their disabilities and difficulties. All need counselling and guidance throughout the phase. There are discontinuities in provision so that some elements of the school curriculum are repeated in post-school courses and there is the lack of a framework for the 14–19 or 21-year period within which individual services can make their contribution. Of course, in a democratic society, it is right that responsibilities rest on parents and young people themselves. But they have access to an education system during the school years which is reasonably intelligible. In the post-compulsory school period there is usually no coherent system and no continuity of concern or provision. They have to shop around, sometimes in a fairly empty market. The development of an orderly system of second phase transition requires joint departmental planning, good cooperation between the professionals and administrators in different services and agencies and a general understanding of the objectives of transition. These objectives need to embrace all aspects of the life of a young adult who is handicapped, not just his capacity to work.

The early adult years

The principal question was posed in the title of an early OECD/CERI study in the United Kingdom written by Patricia

Rowan in 1981. This was published under the title 'What Sort of Life?'[13] The reason for considering this question is because the answers to it should inform the work of special education particularly in the final school years or the first phase of transition. There has been much discussion and writing about community provision; for many young adults the alternative is remaining at home or entering a hospital or institution. There is an increasing range of sheltered housing and group home living, but it is not yet the general rule for those who are handicapped to leave home to live independently like many of their contemporaries. Alternatives to open employment may be unimaginative, and recreational and leisure possibilities limited. Apart from limited resources or a switch of existing resources to new arrangements there are at least three main obstacles to progress. As has been mentioned earlier, many parents are reluctant to let their disabled young adults go. Combinations of responsibility, anxiety and lack of confidence result in fostering dependence long after it is necessary. At the same time the closing of residential institutions is placing burdens on families to care for their young people without always offering reasonable alternatives. Moreover, the home situation and the additional finance parents may receive for looking after their young adults continues to be an obstacle. A second hindrance is in the form of administrative and professional expectations. For reasons that are caring and charitable, many of the young people are thought incapable of independent living. This is in some respects a chicken and egg situation. If they are not thought capable, no training for independence will be provided and, if no training is provided, the young adults cannot demonstrate their potential. But a third significant obstacle is the inertia imposed by existing arrangements. Arrangements satisfactory to professionals are not easily changed without commitment and strong leadership. There is much tradition, prestige and public support for voluntary and statutory institutions and services which are difficult to redirect into new channels. The resources available, being finite, go to maintain existing provision and there is little available for new initiatives. The retraining of personnel and the reallocation of resources which is required is not easy to effect.

However, preparation for transition can at least prepare individuals for a life in which they are capable of useful work, of looking after themselves to the maximum extent and of following leisure interests and recreations. It should envisage the making of long-term personal relationships, including marriage and parenthood. Preparation should certainly not condition young people who are handicapped to be easily satisfied and to accept what is offered without question. Only by aiming high will the necessary skills and attitudes for a full life be developed. Opportunities for development are currently limited, but need not remain so.

Partnership

Among the most important people with whom special educators work are the parents. The development of a real partnership in meeting special educational needs, however, still has a long way to go. As with relationships with other professionals, so too with parents. In the past many professionals have placed the onus on parents to prove they are responsible. Partnership involves accepting that parents are responsible, that they know their children and have something to contribute to a discussion of their needs. This should be assumed unless proved otherwise.

This partnership has been most evident in successful pre-school schemes. Parents have undertaken programmes conscientiously in cooperation with professionals. Indeed the replication of the Portage Scheme in the Wessex Regional Hospital Board Area demonstrated clearly that parents from all social strata were conscientious and effective even during times of considerable tension and difficulties within families. This degree of partnership and commitment is also evident in schemes to help children with reading difficulties such as that reported in Haringay.

Undertaking agreed delegated tasks is perhaps the easiest form of partnership. The most difficult is to accept a parental contribution to the assessment of special educational needs and to the planning of programmes to meet them. This aspect of partnership depends on how parents are introduced to the fact that their child may have such needs, what help they get in understanding the nature of disabilities and difficulties, and how far they are prepared to accept that they exist. Where the causes of learning difficulties are not very obvious it is all too easy for parents to assume that the child's failure is the teacher's fault and equally easy for the teacher to assume it results from home conditions. Within ordinary schools, much depends on the way in which all parents are informed about the work of the school and the kinds of occasions arranged for parents and teachers to meet. The 1980 Education Act recognised that parents need information and specified the general nature of what should be provided, including how the school provides for special educational needs. Given that schools make parents welcome and provide relaxed occasions when they can discuss their children's progress, the important question is when and how schools inform parents that learning difficulties exist. In the past this has often been at too late a stage when other specialists are to be called in and the school has reached the end of its own resources. Partnership can only grow properly when parents know as soon as schools detect a difficulty and when they are asked to contribute their knowledge of the child to early assessment. At the same time many can begin to give extra help in collaboration with teachers.

Teachers are not alone in being prone to tell parents what to do. Other professionals involved in assessment have also had to learn to listen and accept the validity of parental experience, however, badly described. The new legislation and regulations now gives parents a right to give their views, describing the child's needs as they see them, receiving professional reports and arguing or disagreeing with what is proposed. Many will need help to understand their contribution to a partnership from voluntary organisations and professionals. Their contribution to the more complex stages of assessment will be made easier if they have been encouraged to communicate with teachers when their children start school and, in some cases, long before learning difficulties may arise.

The problem of parental counselling during their children's adolescence has already been mentioned. There is another aspect of partnership during these years, which presents some difficulties. Many schools and services will be encouraging young people who are handicapped to think for themselves. They want to encourage a contribution to decision-making. As a result, in some cases, attention is concentrated on the young person to the exclusion of the parent with the understandable aim of encouraging autonomy and independence. Partnership with parents during this phase needs skilled development. They will wish to be involved in planning the future, they will have rights and responsibilities and, in many cases, they will be expected to look after the young person at home during transition to adulthood. They may need help to reduce their child's dependence and to encourage more self-help and independent activity. Excluding them from discussions with their children may be counterproductive. During transition there is a need to transform the parents' role. It is, in fact, another weaning process, involving a subtle change in attitudes and expectations to encourage their children to stand on their own feet as far as possible. This is much more difficult when the disability has necessitated constant attention and reinforced a dependence on others. What emerges, where conditions are favourable, is that the partnership is extended to include the young person. The initial dual partnership of parent and professional becomes a trio involving the adolescent to an increasing extent until he makes an equal contribution.

The development of this participation by young people who are handicapped needs to start early. Choices need to be available as part of education, and decision-making encouraged. This is much more difficult for those with disabilities. Physical disabilities may mean that the child cannot move towards experiences, they have to be brought to him or he has to be taken to them. Children with learning difficulties may find experience confusing unless they are mediated and managed for them to cope with. It has taken years of skilled help to develop a degree of self-advocacy in some schools and adult centres for the mentally handicapped. It can be done successfully but it is still not widespread. All young disabled people need to develop appropriate and socially acceptable self-advocacy skills and special education has a major responsibility in this respect.

With some of those who are handicapped, parents, teachers and care workers may need to reverse their approach. Most ordinary adolescents tend to force the pace as they grow through adolescence, testing limits of acceptance; staying out late, drinking, and exploring sexual relationships are among many of the expressions of the growing awareness of adulthood. Adults naturally tend to slow down the pace of change, to restrain excesses and to slowly release control as personal responsibility develops. The opposite of this approach may be needed where dependence, because of disabilities, has become strong and depression about their long-term effects has resulted in limited drives. Many young disabled people may need positive encouragement to experiment with adult roles, to express their views and to start to carve out their own life style. Positive encouragement is necessary to develop self-advocacy in the partnerships where decisions are taken about the future.

CHAPTER 8

Personnel Preparation and Community Care

In the second half of the twentieth century academic and professional qualifications have increased in number and standards. Apprenticeships and indentures have given way to technical and academic courses in colleges and universities. The content of courses has increased and their length extended. In many respects emphasis has been placed on theory and what to do rather than how to do it. All these trends have been evident in the preparation of those who work with children who are handicapped. Having looked at many of the issues in special education, a major question is how far personnel preparation is changing to meet them. Training programmes, particularly those requiring professional approval, are not easy to change and their response to new conditions in the fields for which they prepare may be slow and hesitant. Is training preparing for the future, preoccupied with the present or even preparing for the past? There is a real danger of qualifying people for kinds of work which no longer exist or are radically changed. A recent example was a special education teachers' course in Norway. Considerable provision is currently made in ordinary schools, yet all the practical teaching experience during the course was carried out in special schools. Thus many of the new skills of cooperative teaching and programme planning in ordinary schools that are now required were not being developed. Such examples are not confined to one country.

In this chapter we turn to professional preparation. Although concentrating on teachers, many of the points are relevant to other professions which contribute to programmes for children who are handicapped. A second major theme is the need for multi-disciplinary training if successful patterns of cooperative work are to become more widespread. It is necessary to look at the current developments in special education and its likely pattern of development if training is to prepare individuals for the changes taking place. These changes affect the work of all teachers, not just those with special education interests and responsibilities.

Initial Training

The tradition in England and Wales has been for most special education teachers to qualify first for primary or secondary teaching, gain some experience and then work in special schools and or take special training courses. It was the 1970 Education Act which resulted in this tradition being questioned. Before the transfer from health to education of responsibility for teaching children with severe degrees of mental retardation, separate initial courses had existed to train for this work. In order to maintain a flow of teachers for this field the courses became incorporated in the teacher training system as initial training with a bias or specialisation in teaching those with mental handicaps. Although the courses produced teachers with qualifications to teach in other sectors, mainly the primary sector, many trainers and students viewed them as an initial special education course. In one sense specialisation to work in special schools and classes became accepted as part of initial training. A similar trend was evident in training teachers of the deaf and, in an increasing number of options under the heading of remedial education, to prepare for work with children with learning difficulties. These trends were often reinforced by the attitudes of students who had an early commitment to work with children who had special educational needs and wished to specialise as early as possible. The extent to which preparation to teach children, deemed to need special education, should be undertaken during initial training remains a major question for debate.

There are at least three major considerations which arise from new developments in special education consequent upon the 1981 Education Act. These suggest that the whole question of initial training will need further discussion. They are:

(a)   the restatement of the responsibilities of primary and

secondary schools for the detection, assessment and provision for children with special educational needs;

(b)   the changing pattern of special education which results in
more provision in ordinary schools, peripatetic advisory
services and collaborative patterns of work with ordinary
teachers;

(c)   the closer incorporation of special education services into
the education service for all children with the increasing
need for joint planning of the curriculum by ordinary and
special education teachers.

The first of these considerations has implications for the initial
training of all teachers and also for the in-service training of
qualified teachers. The other two concern the training of special
education teachers and not only bear on the question of their
initial training but also on subsequent specialised training.

Initial Training for All in Special Education Needs

The Warnock Report recommended that an element concerned
with special educational needs should form part of initial teacher
training courses and indicated some of the ingredients of such an
element. Since that time many training institutions have attempted to develop this aspect of their courses, but there are a number
of difficulties particularly in the limited time available during one
year postgraduate training. Expressed simply, the problem became a matter of what could be left out if anything new was to be
added. But again there was a tendency to see special education as
an addition to ordinary education and not as a relative emphasis
within ordinary education. Special education skills are still to
some extent seen as different and separate rather than as an
extended development of good teaching skills. It is necessary to
develop a conceptual framework similar to that outlined in
respect of the school's responses in chapter 6.

The first important point is how far ordinary teacher training
courses prepare for work with the range of individual differences
in learning styles, learning skills and background experiences
normally found in schools. To be more specific, how far do
courses for primary school teachers develop skills of class management and grouping, together with appropriate task setting so
that less successful learners can make progress?. How far do
courses for secondary subject teachers include attention to the
objectives, methods and materials that are likely to be most

effective with those with below average attainments, who may be slower to learn and who may have been relatively unsuccessful in primary schools? If these major considerations, which may affect between thirty to forty per cent of the schools population, receive insufficient emphasis, then less severe learning difficulties may become special educational needs. The gap between ordinary and special education will increase and more special provision will be needed.

It can be argued that teacher training still makes too many assumptions about all children being motivated active learners. Marked failure to learn is nearly always attributed to intrinsic flaws in the child's cognitive processes. Too little attention is given to identifying the conditions under which less effective learners could make the most progress. Special education has now demonstrated the value of teachers with the ability to analyse learning tasks, to set clear and practical objectives and to plan orderly and sequential programmes to achieve them. But these are general teaching skills not exclusive to special education. Teachers with these skills often achieve greater job satisfaction as small gains are achieved and planned teaching is recognised as effective. These general skills, derived from special education experience, should become an integral part of initial training for all teachers. As a result, work with less effective learners may become more rewarding.

Another vital aspect of the work of all teachers is the assessment and recording of each pupil's progress. It is important that the identification of and assessment of special educational needs should grow out of a school's general procedures for recording its pupils' progress and not be seen as a separate specialist field. All teachers need some skills in evaluating children's work and keeping practical records on which to plan future work. The change from record keeping as a history to record keeping as an essential element in developing teaching programmes is taking place. The more effective it is for all children, the less may need to be added to identify learning difficulties and assess special needs of all kinds. If this aspect of work is dealt with imaginatively within initial training programmes less time may need to be devoted to assessment in any special education element of the course.

It is, therefore, suggested that an essential pre-requisite for planning a specific special education input is a review of initial training courses as a whole. This review should pay particular attention to the preparation given to equip teachers to work with relatively inefficient learners who constitute about one third of all the children they teach. This preparation should include studying appropriate curriculum variants, considering and selecting essential skills and ideas, and looking at materials and methods for this section of the school population. Expectations should be high but practicable in the time available. It should also include assessment and record keeping, task analysis, goal setting and programme planning. This review may also require a further look at the relative time and attention devoted to developing students' own academic excellence and helping them to acquire essential practical teaching skills if the less academic child is to receive the right quality of teaching.

The nature and the scope of the special education input is thus very dependent on the priorities which determine the initial training course as a whole and, at best, grows naturally from essential elements in it. It is not proposed to discuss the special education input in detail since much will depend on the structure of degree courses and postgraduate diplomas. Some implications of the changes in special education, already outlined, need, however, to be borne in mind.

The growing complexity in the range of special educational provision means that what is done during initial training can only be an introduction to be followed up by later in-service training. It is far more important to concentrate on the more common kinds of special educational needs met by most teachers than to attempt to deal with rarer and more complex disabilities and difficulties. Particularly important is a sound and detailed discussion of the possible ways in which primary and secondary schools may provide for children with significant learning difficulties who are not the subject of statements. Good models exist, but few have been written up and the whole rationale of such provision needs further development. However, a lack of material should not prevent a study of the problems. Arrangements in local schools can be studied by students and some of the main principles on which arrangements should be made derived from such studies.

It is also important that major issues in provision for those who are handicapped should be tackled. The process of integration, its history, its social context and its implications for schools is one example. Initial training provides a unique opportunity to build on general studies of the social setting of education, of child development, of learning, and of social interaction in schools by focusing on a specific topic. The future development of special education will be helped considerably by a teaching force that is well informed about one of its major preoccupations. Another example is the transition from school to adult life. Teachers in secondary schools need to be aware of what faces their pupils when they leave, particularly those with limited academic achievements. To look at the problems facing young people with disabilities can illuminate this process of transition for a significant proportion of the school population. This, therefore, can be another useful focus for discussing elements in initial training such as the curriculum, counselling and guidance, vocational preparation and the development of social and life skills.

Assuming that the special education input will also build on general courses covering assessment and recording, task analysis and programme planning, it should take these further and indicate what might need to be added to identify and meet special educational needs. To do this will also involve knowledge of the work of other services which visit schools to help with assessment and provision such as health services, social services, psychological services and peripatetic teaching services. This knowledge should include good models as well as current local practices which may not always be well developed.

Finally, considerable emphasis has already been placed on collaboration, cooperative patterns of work and co-teaching. Again, a study of this topic in respect of special education can build on work in the course as a whole where this looks critically at school organisation, team teaching and curriculum development. Meeting many special educational needs in future will depend on ordinary and special education teachers working together. The time when a learning problem was handed over to be cured is long passed. So should be the attitudes which encourage ordinary teachers to think that all such problems can only be dealt with by specialists. Joint planning and cooperative teaching are essential in many current forms of provision and they should they should be introduced during initial training.

The special education input in initial training can take many forms. It can be a separate course or elements in other courses. In practice it is sometimes difficult to know what is going on in a complex array of modules and courses taught by different departments and specialists. The training institution needs a coherent plan which is not simply added on but is a natural development of general preparation. The plan should include those aspects of special education which all students should study, with optional courses for those who wish to start developing a special interest in the field.

The arguments in this section are based on two propositions. The first is that the new responsibilities of all ordinary schools, for the detection, assessment and provision for children with special educational needs, requires that all teachers have some awareness of the means of meeting these responsibilities. This awareness should start from their initial training. The second is the relative definition of special educational needs, already argued, which requires that ordinary and special education issues are closely related. Training should not separate them unnecessarily but should be devised to examine the common ground between ordinary and special needs and ordinary and special programmes.

Specialisation during initial training

This issue has already been outlined briefly. It is being developed here as an aspect of the third consideration, namely, the changed pattern of special educational provision. It is natural for students to want to make an early commitment to work with children who are handicapped, especially where during the final years of schooling they have done voluntary work and become engaged in the problems to be solved. It is equally evident that, where a special education system is envisaged as consisting mainly of separate special schools, preparation to work in those schools at an early stage would seem a logical approach. Traditional ideas about categories of handicap and long-term placements in special schools reinforce these views. Training to teach a class in a special school for a particular disability appears to be a clear-cut task.

Of course much depends on what is meant by specialisation. Initial training provides the basic qualification to teach in ordinary primary and secondary schools if a period of probationary teaching is successfully completed. Should there be initial teacher training courses which result in a special education qualification such as a teacher of deaf children or of mentally handicapped children? It is argued that there should not be such courses and that all teachers whatever their eventual fields of work should have followed a course which qualified them to teach in ordinary schools. This does not mean that there cannot or should not be special education options in initial courses but these should only add knowledge and skills to the ordinary qualification.

The initial reasons for taking this view were very general. Teaching children with disabilities and difficulties required more skills and it was better to establish competence with ordinary children first. Successful experience in primary or secondary schools gives a useful insight into learning and teaching on which to build further training. It also establishes credibility in the teaching force which enhances the status of special education. It gives teachers in special education an idea of the standards of achievement reached by children of different ages and thus a useful yardstick in setting goals and evaluating progress in special education.

These reasons are still sound but there are now others. Special educational provision now includes more special classes and units in ordinary schools. More special schools are acting as resource centres working closely with primary and secondary schools. More special education teachers are working in peripatetic advisory roles. In effect, special and ordinary education are becoming more closely interrelated. There are very few disabilities, including severe degrees of mental retardation, where some provision is not made in primary and secondary schools. This type of arrangement is likely to increase in the future. To be effective it requires close cooperation between special education teachers and the staff of the host schools. The former should be knowledgeable about the work of ordinary schools, the conditions and restraints under which teachers work and the curriculum they teach. The success of new patterns of work will depend on mutual understanding and respect which will be enhanced where special education teachers demonstrate their ability to teach ordinary classes. A period of experience in ordinary schools before undertaking special education training and teaching is, therefore, becoming more and more important.

In-Service Training

The developing pattern of special education has very significant implications for in-service training in two main areas. These are the training of all qualified teachers in post about special educational needs and provision, and the specialist training of those qualified teachers who are to staff the new range of arrangements for children with disabilities and significant difficulties. These implications spring from the three major considerations outlined at the beginning of this chapter.

The training of all qualified teachers presents formidable problems because of the numbers involved. There have been important initiatives including new one-term courses and local education authority schemes (such as those in Oxfordshire and the SNAP programme in Coventry). It is not proposed to discuss the form of in-service training except in one respect, since there will be many local variations. The main points to be made will concern the objectives and context of such training.

The one aspect of training which needs further attention is the question of separate courses or elements in other courses. The main approach is to develop separate courses dealing with special educational needs. These sessional, short- and long-term courses attract many teachers concerned with the learning and behaviour difficulties they commonly face. In the main they have been devised and run by special educators and educational psychologists and have focused on the causes of difficulties and special approaches to overcome them. What is less common is the insertion of elements or sessions in other courses where the relationship between ordinary and special needs can be studied. For example, in curriculum-oriented courses for primary and secondary teachers, there may be considerable advantages in looking at the needs of less successful learners and those identified as having special educational needs together. Such an approach can help teachers to identify what can be done within the ordinary teaching programme to cater for different rates and styles of learning, and what might be needed in addition for some children. In can also look at practicable forms of cooperative activities between ordinary and special education teachers. The diploma course in mathematics for the low achiever, jointly developed by the Mathematical Association and the National Association for Remedial Education, is a good example of a major course of this kind. The same principles need to be applied to a wider range of curriculum courses so that special educational considerations are seen to be an integral part of primary and secondary teaching and not simply an additional area of study. Similarly courses for head teachers and senior staff on the management of schools should include special educational needs among the range of special needs which have to be considered in planning the work of schools. This study will be helped where local education authorities have developed a policy for meeting special educational needs in ordinary schools and can provide senior staff with some possible models for arrangements which they are prepared to support.

This leads to the first point about content. Although it will be important to look at the nature of disabilities and difficulties to see how they arise and what effects they may have on learning, it is equally important to help teachers develop a conceptual framework for considering special education. As has already been said, many current arrangements have been built up in an *ad hoc* way to meet immediate problems. The 1981 Act provided some useful outlines for developing more coherent approaches and these need debate and development within in-service training. In other words, the ordinary teacher undergoing these forms of in-service training should end up with a reasonably clear idea of the close relationship of ordinary to special education, the main lines on which authorities are developing provision and the pattern of advisory and supportive services available. He should also gain an insight into the nature of significant learning difficulties of all kinds and how the first steps can be taken to deal with them.

A second point also concerns specialist preparation. Many of the arrangements made, including the new approaches of many special schools, involve collaboration between ordinary and special education teachers. Forms of working should be explored in in-service training. These may take a number of forms, such as the class teacher supervising a programme developed by the special education teacher, but some of the most effective arrangements include joint planning and co-teaching. What are the best ways for the two teachers concerned to decide on objectives, select or develop teaching materials and devise appropriate means for children to record their experiences? What is the most effective use of time if both are working in the same classroom? Where special education is provided part-time outside the ordinary classroom, what arrangements are necessary to coordinate work in both settings, share experience and evaluate progress? Right at the outset, in introductory courses for primary and secondary teachers, it seems important to demonstrate that special educational needs are a shared concern. Medical models implying that others cure them need to be discouraged and the ordinary teacher's ability to make a useful contribution reinforced.

One important aspect of this area of training is the actual case material used on the courses. There are obvious advantages if the teachers can study the problems of individual children they teach. Most people need to work with concrete examples and many aspects of special educational needs can be made clear through real experiences. Shortages of time and other factors can lead to an over-emphasis on lectures about different disabilities and difficulties which individuals may find hard to relate to their own experiences in the classroom. The great danger is that courses of this kind might increase knowledge and understanding without helping the student to devise practical steps to solve the problems he faces. Much of the content of in-service courses could usefully be drawn from teachers' study of their own schools and children with learning difficulties. Tutors can then build on this experience to develop both practical programmes and general principles.

School based in-service training is one means of achieving this. Video tapes illustrating learning difficulties and micro-teaching studies can also help. There is a great need for material of this kind to engage the teacher in planning to meet recognisable problems.

Specialist in-service training

Preparation for teachers to work in special education normally falls under this heading although in effect it is *post qualification initial training*. In this respect it is similar to other courses which build on basic teaching experience such as those for school counsellors and careers guidance teachers. The field is a complex one with full-time and part-time courses, diplomas and higher degrees, and college based or distance learning courses. Some courses have developed to prepare for teaching children with specific disabilities such as visual and hearing handicaps. Others have attempted to deal with a wide variety of disabilities and difficulties with a series of options. Some have been required qualifications, as in the case of teachers of the deaf and blind, others have not. All have been subject to change and increasing pressure to raise academic standards as they sought validation by universities and the CNAA. However, this is not the context in which to discuss the pattern of training in detail. The recent report by a working party of the Advisory Committee on the Supply and Training of Teachers has covered this ground. What is attempted in the following paragraphs is to comment on a number of issues which arise from the increasing range of tasks in special education and the way in which training does or should prepare for them.

The major change has been the new variety of situations in which special education teachers may work. Most of the long established courses began with the expectation that students would take a post in special schools. They would teach a class of children placed in a particular category of handicap and take further responsibilities in a school for that handicap. Courses were aimed at preparing for one category of special school or for work in remedial classes and groups in ordinary schools. But a new range of situations has emerged and a new range of skills is necessary. It is now recognised that a significant proportion of the special education population has more than one disability or difficulty. Many more children who would have attended special schools are being educated in special classes in ordinary schools and a variety of units elsewhere. The age range of special education has now extended from seven to fifteen years between six months and nineteen years. Many programmes involve close cooperation with parents and other professions. Much closer collaboration with ordinary teachers is also essential in many situations. What influence should these changes have on the future development of special education teacher training?

There are many practical problems which influence current provision, such as limited resources to second teachers to full-time courses and the increasing emphasis on part-time courses. Most teachers also prefer to live at home while taking courses because of the costs of living away from home. At the same time it is difficult to establish a network which ensures that all geographical regions have a reasonable range of courses and that the strengths of different training institutions are used effectively. These and a number of other difficulties have been discussed by the Association of Special Education Teacher Trainers and by other bodies. Some solutions have been found, for example the distance teaching approach of the Birmingham University part-time course for teachers of the visually handicapped, while research into a modular approach in the North West of England has looked at others. Again, because practical problems and their solutions change, it is not intended to do more than recognise their importance.

It may be helpful to start with one example of how a system of courses has been built up in Norway.[14] Training is provided at three levels. Part I is offered in teachers' colleges and in a part-time form. It aims to give an introduction to basic training in special education which includes the framework of special educational provision, factors contributing to disabilities and learning difficulties, observation and assessment, special educational methods and curriculum studies. This one-year course or its part-time equivalent is recognised as a first qualification in special education and aims at preparation for the wide range of common special educational needs in ordinary schools. Part II builds on Part I and is a course emphasising the practical aspects of teaching in a particular field. These may include: maladjustment, visual disability, hearing disability, multiple handicap, learning disabilities or speech and communication disorders. This course, originally of one year's full-time duration or its part-time equivalent, has been extended by an extra year devoted to preventive work, cooperation and collaboration with other professionals as well as an extension of work with individuals who are handicapped. The aim of Part III – of which entry requirement is the successful completion of the first year of Part II – is to give students a general knowledge of social science research methods and develop basic skills for research and evaluation in special education. The middle of the two-year course is mainly devoted to a special research project and the final semester to preparing for the work which students will undertake after the course. Thus the framework provides a progression from the general to the specific and from a broad knowledge, through specific fields, to important general skills and principles.

The illustration is important since it shows how all the major training needs are met in sequence. First, there is a common basis for all special education teachers which provides a basis for work in ordinary schools; secondly, there is preparation for particular kinds of work, now being extended by an extra year to include problems of integration and collaboration; and finally there is provision for planning, management and research roles in the development of special education. The present position in England and Wales is that all this is usually compressed into a single one-year full-time course or a part-time alternative. Although there is an increase in higher degree possibilities of the Part III kind, most training courses either attempt Part I or Part II, while giving some attention, in both, to research and to individual studies and projects. But it is the Norwegian example which gives the clearest framework for meeting current and developing training needs.

An important factor to bear in mind is that the amount of training needed should be related to the incidence and complexity of special educational needs. The greater incidence of less severe and complex learning difficulties in ordinary schools requires the greatest training provision. A much smaller group of teachers is required to work with specific severe disabilities and difficulties and fewer still are needed to develop and manage the special education system and to become teacher trainers. Does the current pattern of courses reflect this principle?

A second principle is that specialisation in one field, such as teaching the hearing impaired, is built on a foundation of knowledge and experience of both ordinary education and general special education. Thus all specialists at this level of work have the same foundation and have followed common courses on which to build. With few exceptions specialist courses may be isolated even in the same institution. It is only relatively recently that the four courses in the University of Birmingham for visual, hearing and learning difficulties and maladjustment have been coordinated so that a common core is developed for all of them. Many other courses remain the separate territories of their tutors.

Many courses attempt to provide for too many levels. Among the students recruited are those who wish to be equipped to work with learning and behaviour difficulties in ordinary schools and those who wish to specialise in work in a particular field such as moderate or severe learning difficulties. Although options are planned, time is limited and it is doubtful if either need is met successfully in many cases.

Finally, the need for course approval by Universities or the CNAA results in significant emphasis on academic studies in different disciplines which are acceptable within the course frameworks for diplomas. This means that studies which might be spread over a longer period in a hierarchy of courses have to be squeezed into a single academic year or its equivalent.

The question of the structure of courses and the way they relate to one another is the first major issue. Can the existing pattern be changed to provide a progression from initial practical proficiency to theoretical and managerial competence? Can the isolated elements be integrated into a coherent structure of national, regional and local courses which reflect both the incidence of special educational needs and the distribution of special education teachers to meet them?

Within this structure of full-time and part-time courses there will need to be new elements to prepare for the changes taking place. These new elements may be included within existing courses or form the core of new ones. Among these elements will be attention to different age ranges, skills to work with parents, co-teaching skills, advisory skills and the problems of integrating the work of units with that of the schools in which they are placed.

The question of age ranges now has two additional aspects to the primary and secondary age ranges which have already been dealt with. The special education of very young children in collaboration with their parents at home, in nurseries and play-groups and in nursery schools and classes is a particular field of work where more attention is needed as the HMI Survey[10] indicates. This report endorses the fact that courses on educational provision and programmes for under fives with special educational needs are one of the most important requirements if this field of work is to continue to develop. Whether there should be special one-year courses, or a series of short courses is a matter for debate, but within the field of special education teacher training this age range receives only limited attention. The other additional element is the sixteen to nineteen plus age range. Whether provision is in ordinary or special schools or ordinary or special colleges of further education, the nature of the curriculum and the essential elements in preparation for adult and working life require further attention. Any courses or parts of courses devoted to this age range must also bear in mind the effects of 16–19 provision on the secondary curriculum. Traditionally, many courses have looked at 14–16 programmes to prepare for school leaving. These programmes will need revision to prepare for further education and training so that there is continuity. Indeed, one approach would be to see the 14–19 curriculum as a coherent element in courses. The extension of the age range raises the question of whether any one course can reasonably encompass the 0–19 age range and if not what age groupings would be most appropriate.

There is a tendency to assume that working with parents is only essential in the early years. When those who are handicapped reach adolescence the focus should be on the individual, not his parents, if independence is to be fostered. However, it is during the period of adolescence and transition from school that most parents feel the need for help. This is not simply a question of advice but, as has been already mentioned, it is often a question of sustained counselling to develop autonomy and more independent lives. Such counselling requires skills for which training is desirable. Certainly courses covering the older age ranges should include this aspect of work with parents in their programme.

Co-teaching and advisory teaching skills have already been stressed as important elements in the future development of special education. How far they are prepared for in training is still uncertain. It is difficult to find time to prepare for effective teaching in special schools and classes and co-teaching and advisory teaching in the same course. There is, perhaps, a case for looking at separate courses for the latter for established special education teachers who wish to move into work with ordinary teachers in the situations already outlined. The problems of co-teaching cannot be dealt with in isolation. Some training is needed for the other partner. Assuming that the special education teacher is to work in a primary or secondary classroom for a number of periods each week, a relationship involving trust and mutual respect has to be built up. Planning the programme together, arranging to share activities and preparing lessons and materials requires time and knowledge of each other's work. It is possible to discuss the ideas in special education teachers' courses but more difficult to develop opportunities to foster good practices. These may require special courses at local level. Advisory teaching involves many of the same skills exercised in less frequent periods in the child's classroom. Both these kinds of work are likely to be undertaken by special education teachers and should be included in their training.

Many more special education teachers now work in relatively isolated special classes and units in ordinary schools. Their numbers are likely to increase. They will lack the direction and leadership given by the head teachers of special schools and may be left to their own resources for long periods. Without preparation they may retreat into the special class and develop few co-operative activities with their colleagues in the host school. These kinds of teaching situation need to be analysed during training and successful methods of integrating a class into a school discussed.

In summary, this brief review of issues for future development, has been selective. It has recognised that the strengths of existing courses continue to be the understanding of individual learning difficulties which result from disabilities of all kinds, the planning of programmes to meet them and the background theoretical studies necessary to provide a basis for the students' professional development. It has suggested that the pattern and structure of special education teacher training should be reviewed, and it has also discussed aspects of developments in special education which need to be included in training if it is to prepare for a changing pattern of service delivery.

Multi-Professional Training

Each profession in the health and social services has a similar problem to that of the teaching profession, namely, to create awareness about children's disabilities and significant difficulties among all its members and to prepare those members who will specialise in work with such children. In practice, specialists in one profession will work with specialists in others and non-specialists in their own and other professions. This makes for a complex pattern of training needs among which to set multi-professional training.

There are a number of general points it is necessary to make before looking at multi-professional or inter-disciplinary training. The generalist-specialist balance is one of them. Experience in the social services has shown that a generic approach to training and work is not successful in a field where there are many similarities to education. There has been a return to building specialisms on a strong common core of training. There have been similar moves in special education to develop generic workers with maladjusted and behaviourally disturbed children and young people. These are workers who combine teaching and care functions. There may be isolated instances in which generalists and dually qualified professionals can make a contribution, but in most cases there are stronger arguments for a single specialist role. Nevertheless, it is now recognised that this needs to be developed on a broad base of general training. This is a similar approach to that suggested for special education teacher training.

Another factor to take into account is the basis on which multi-professional cooperation and training is likely to be most effective. Experience would tend to show that a person should be secure in his own professional role if he is to function effectively with others. It is often uncertainty or indeed wrong assumptions about one's own professional boundaries which coupled with ignorance about those of others', leads to difficulties. Similarly, it is necessary to recognise what services can be provided either by oneself or by the department to which one belongs. These points can be illustrated by the ecological approach to assessment put forward by Nicholas Hobbs.[3] This suggests that assessment should end up with a specification of individual needs and a clear identification of who is to meet them or arrange for them to be met. Thus, within the health service, medical treatment could be arranged by the doctor, nursing by the nurse and therapy by the appropriate therapist. In the social services those specialising in work with the handicapped could provide necessary support and those responsible for fostering and adoption would operate where these arrangements were proposed. Within the education services similar differentiations would occur. The 1981 Act and the procedures for making statements follow this pattern. Only educational administrators can decide in which of the schools or units a child will be placed with the parents' agreement. Other professionals may identify needs but only offer or arrange the kinds of treatment, thereapy or teaching they can provide. Thus, a prerequisite for multi-professional working is a definition of individual professional functions and a sensitive awareness of how they relate to each other.

The first steps in preparation should take place during initial training, and it is important that tutors should themselves be well informed about other professions. Their attitudes to multi-professional work are also vital since those in training are very influenced by their trainers. Questions need to be asked in each training sector. In paediatrics and general practice training how are the important features of children's education and the provision of special education presented and by whom? The same question can be asked about social work training and in teacher training: how is child health and social service provision presented? It is because basic attitudes to multi-professional work are laid down, together with stereotypes of other professions, that more attention needs to be given to this aspect of initial training.

Many aspects of multi-professional work such as assessment, case conferences and planning involve chairmanship and leadership. Unless individuals are secure in their roles, and the contributions of different services are accorded respect, tensions arise. Team work may be inhibited by personalities, prejudices and struggles for a dominant role. Many of the same problems influence the initiation of multi-professional training. Sensitivity about status and inter-service tensions may result in initiatives from one service or department of a training institution, being misinterpreted as challenges for leadership. It is sometimes difficult to find a body or individual regarded as neutral to set up courses and conferences.

In practice, the best setting for learning about the work of others and how one's own professional skills can fit into team working is day-to-day experience. This means that regular meetings need to be planned to discuss individual special educational needs. Although individual professional assessments, followed by written reports, may be a more efficient use of time, unless there are discussions over time in meetings, insight into the concerns of other professionals may be slow to develop. It is suggested that team-working arrangements need to be seen as having an important multi-professional training element and that time needs to be devoted to sharing general information and knowledge as well as discussing individual cases.

There remains a need, however, for courses of all kinds where different professionals can come together and discuss common problems away from the pressures of day-to-day work and decision-making. Such courses are probably more effective when individuals have had some specialist training and work experience. A number of different levels of course should be envisaged including occasions when field workers can study day-to-day problems of assessment, programme planning and service delivery, and opportunities for managers of different services to look at the coordination of professional work.

In countries like the United Kingdom where responsibilities are delegated to local authorities and districts, forms of training depend on local circumstances. No attempt is being made to suggest a particular form of training. All that is being advocated here is the acknowledgement of multi-professional in-service training as an essential element in developing new procedures for assessing special educational needs and planning to meet them. It is particularly important if professional preoccupations with status and territories of operation are not to distort arrangements to the detriment of individuals who are handicapped and their families.

Community Care

At first sight the preparation of local communities to integrate individuals who are handicapped may not appear to be a training problem. However it is in two particular senses. One is the training of all professionals who work in the field to be aware of what the community can offer and how ordinary citizens can contribute to the quality of life of those who are disabled. The second is the way in which community resources can be developed to include them in the normal pattern of work, leisure and domestic life. Voluntary organisations of all kinds also play a significant part in developing awareness of special needs and of the contribution ordinary people can make.

Money is easier to give than time and it is unfortunate that the real need for money by voluntary organisations, special schools and other institutions often dominates the approach in local communities. It is very easy for the individual to assume that this is all that is needed and 'they' will provide everything else. The ability to raise money also reflects a pecking order within chairty groups. Voluntary organisations and special schools for the visually impaired, physically disabled and mentally handicapped are better supported than organisations and schools for slow learners or emotional and behaviour problems. There is a real need for voluntary financial contributions to enhance public services and to fill gaps in them. It is unfortunate that different special interests compete and that other kinds of potential contribution are less effectively mobilised.

The competition for attention from different organisations and schools concerned with particular disabilities and difficulties is also unfortunate in another respect. A coherent approach to policy development at national and local level and to public education about handicapping effects is seldom evident, and special interests are pursued to the detriment of shared concerns. It is to be hoped that in future a more coordinated effort will be made by those concerned with the field of disability and handicap to educate the public and to harness voluntary contributions of all kinds. This will require a greater emphasis on the common needs of children and young people considered handicapped and on general arrangements to help them in local communities.

Some initiatives are evident. Radio programmes such as 'In Touch' and 'Does he Take Sugar?' reach a relatively wide audience. Similarly, television programmes can also create awareness. Perhaps more can be done in adult education. Certainly there could be a change in emphasis, when many different local organisations are approached, to ask for time not money. But the major problem in most instances is the ignorance, apprehension and uncertainty of the average person who has had no contact with disability. That is why the development of integrative activities during the school years is so important. Young children and young people soon develop healthy attitudes to handicaps when exposed to them and when the adults who work with them are well disposed to share experiences.

In the USA one example of a community approach which illustrates a number of points is the Association for Retarded Citizens in St Louis, Missouri. Among a range of services offered by this association, the Assistance with Respite Care in the Home (ARCH) scheme provides short-term relief care for families of mentally retarded and developmentally disabled children and adults. A paid supervisor trains volunteers who are available to families who make their own financial and other arrangements with them. The team of volunteers is available twenty four hours a day, seven days a week, and families may contract for different periods and kinds of help. Where families cannot afford expenses for volunteers, subsidies are available. All volunteers have back-up emergency support from the ARCH supervisor. In the first three months of 1983, 250 families were provided with 13,000 hours of respite care. The important lessons to be learned from this example are that volunteers were available. They were given training and support but they were encouraged to make direct links with families and individuals who are handicapped. Some financial recompense for their time was available. They also had links with the Association's other services which included recreational and leisure activities. Thus, this particular scheme is educating the community in the attitudes, approaches and techniques which enhance community care at a relatively small cost, namely a supervisor's salary and subsidies via the local social services for a minority of families. Respite Care helps some families to overcome the isolation that is often associated with the care of a disabled member and to have more contact with friends, neighbours and community organisations.

The Youth Service is often sensitive to disability and such arrangements as PHAB clubs (Physically Handicapped Able Bodies) do valuable work. Gateway Clubs for those with mental handicaps are also important introductions into social life, as are the clubs run by special schools. Those who are disabled, particularly the profoundly deaf, need to spend time with each other to share tensions and problems and relax away from the pressures of integrated activities. So there needs to be a balance in community preparation which makes access easy to shared facilities and activities, but also accords special groups for those who are disabled the same status and respect as other groups. Poverty has been defined as lack of choice; the social life of a young disabled adult can be impoverished if there is a lack of choice. If the close association of ordinary and special education is to continue to develop there must be seen to be a similarly close association between different forms of community provision for continuing education, recreation and social association. This is an educational task which is now recognised but which continues to need attention.

CHAPTER 9

The Way Ahead

The way ahead for special education is not clearly defined although in the United Kingdom legislation has provided a new basis on which to make progress. There are still important choices to be made and priorities to be determined at national, local authority and school levels. In a field where sectional interests, expediency and *ad hoc* responses to immediate problems have traditionally been dominant, there is now a need for a comprehensive approach integrated within policies for education as a whole. The purpose of this chapter is to identify critical factors which should inform choices and to suggest an agenda for the future.

Significant Factors

The increasing use of new technologies and changing political and social policies are two factors which have always influenced special education but which in the next two decades may be expected to have more dramatic effects on the kind of provision made for those deemed handicapped. The proportion of available resources devoted by developed countries to the care, education, technological and other support of disadvantaged citizens and minority groups will be crucial.

Technology

Major changes in the development of new technologies will not only include the introduction of more and more sophisticated micro-electronic hardware and software to domestic, commercial, industrial and recreational activities but also their application to effective teaching and training practices. The positive and negative aspects of these for those who are handicapped will need to be recognised particularly in preparing for their transition to adult and working life. Indeed, a radical change in the pattern of living and working is likely for everybody. New systems will influence banking, shopping, entertainment and, more significantly, the range of employment opportunities. Information processing will eliminate some jobs and create fewer, particularly in middle management, to replace them. Routine manufacturing jobs will be replaced by more sophisticated machines. More complex communications systems may replace direct human contact. The labour market will change and daily life for many will alter as new technology exerts its influence. The concept of full employment will need revision and possibly replacement with a concept of useful work and a social wage as the wealth of communities is produced by fewer and fewer productive workers. The effects for those who are disabled or have significant difficulties will be considerable. On the positive side there is evidence of better environmental control, of easier access to aspects of the curriculum in education and of improved means of communication. A wider variety of work may be available both as a result of more effective education and training and because new technologies will make jobs easier for those with disabilities to undertake. Major disadvantages may result from a reduced labour market in which those who are handicapped may have fewer opportunities and experience a more impersonal approach to their needs as terminals replace human contacts for many day-to-day transactions. On balance, there should be more advantages than disadvantages where technology can give to the individual who is handicapped more control and more choice over communication, learning, mobility and living arrangements.

In the field of communication, advances will continue to be made in hearing aids for those who are deaf. These aids will be more selective in their amplification, and visual display associated with computers and with personal aids will enable communication and language development to be enhanced. Similarly, it is a reasonable expectation that those who are blind will be able to have aids which turn speech into written language and which in turn make written language more readily available through speech. Finally, those with severe physical disabilities will have more effective hardware to facilitate mobility and communication. All these advances may also have applications for individuals with learning difficulties. We may reasonably expect that the future will bring easier means of receptive and responsive verbal communication to many who are disabled.

Environmental control devices will also increase in sophistication. Although these will have major implications for independent living they will also influence education. Aids to mobility for those who are blind, visual cues for those who are deaf and a whole range of technology to improve mobility for those with physical disabilities are on the way. Remote control devices will enable the latter to open and shut doors, switch equipment on and off and select appropriate media presentations. As a result, special education which has traditionally brought experience to children who are handicapped, and teachers who have controlled the material available will be able to offer more choice, more independent action and study and more control over what is learned to the children and young people they teach.

Effective learning can also be enhanced by properly programmed equipment which offers the continued practice of skills beyond most teachers' patience. Similarly, it will be possible for those students who find it hard to keep written records to have access to a memory in which personal experiences and notes are readily available. Together with the improved facilities for communication, these new aids to individual learning should enable the curriculum to be developed and learning to be increased in speed and efficiency.

Finally, micro-technology can increase access to many aspects of the curriculum which have traditionally been hard to teach to children with limited sensory abilities and physical skills. Micro-computer programmes can improve access to science, the humanities, language and literature, among other areas of study, by providing the student with access and choice and by enhancing experience through auditory and visual channels.

It is a reasonable expectation that new technology will revolutionise teaching those with disabilities and significant difficulties. It can also make a major contribution to assessment, record keeping and report writing. Once teaching objectives are defined precisely and the programmes to meet them developed, these can be translated into individual records of progress on computers into which day-to-day evidence of progress can be readily fed. Linked with a word-processor individual reports can then be produced easily and rapidly. Programmes to produce the Individual Educational Programmes required in the USA have already been developed on an experimental basis. Many of the time-consuming assessment and review procedures necessary as a result of the 1981 Education Act will become much simpler to manage once current technology development projects have produced the means to do so.

All the elements discussed in the previous paragraphs exist and new ones are a reasonable expectation. The significance for special education will be great. First the development and management of individual programmes initiated within the curriculum framework of the school will be facilitated. Secondly, the quality of programmes will be enhanced since it will be possible for the best to be made more widely available. Thirdly, the process of integration into ordinary schools may be speeded up since it will be easier to provide appropriate programmes and materials in settings less dependent on day-to-day contact with specialist teachers. Finally, the curriculum for many children with special education may be enriched by easier access to some areas of study. To achieve this will require training in new techniques and in the use of software, but it will free special education from many restraints. Time devoted to individuals may be increased as routine practice activities are transferred to self-managed programmes which are self-correcting. Individual studies will be more easy to plan as children and young people have access to a wider range of material in forms they can assimilate. Teachers can be expected to become planners and managers of learning in addition to their inspirational and motivational role and not the primary teaching machines which they have had to be.

Teaching Technology

The effect of a systematic analysis of tasks to be learned, of sequences of objectives and of learning experiences are yet to be fully recognised. Work with individuals with severe disabilities and severe degrees of learning impairment has shown that expectations can be higher. For example, the programme that enabled a young woman with Downs Syndrome, last measured IQ 30, to hold down open employment in a hotel is not simply a tribute to her response. It is the outcome of sophisticated teaching technology. Similarly, the young people with marked degrees of mental retardation capable of accurate laboratory testing work, demonstrate what can be achieved by a systematic analysis of work and by skilled training. Neither of these examples are soulless examples of conditioning and both enable individuals to have higher opinions of themselves and to exercise choice.

A more widespread use of techniques that have already been developed would have a major impact on special education.

However, they demand skilled teachers, an imaginative exploration of opportunities available in the community and higher expectations. Longer periods of education are needed than are often available in the United Kingdom and a more systematic approach to the curriculum, particularly during the period from thirteen or fourteen years or age to the early twenties. It is important that these new techniques are made available not only in the education programmes offered to disabled individuals, but also in the teacher training programmes.

Political and Social Trends

These are never easy to forecast despite their significance for policies which influence minorities, among which are groups classed as handicapped. A major current trend is the polarisation of the radical right and the militant left, neither of whom find the middle ground acceptable. It seems reasonable to argue that the most marked advance in attitudes towards those with disabilities and significant difficulties occurred when there was a consensus in the middle ground. During the previous three decades changes of government did not seriously affect progress towards according more rights to those who were handicapped. A process of normalisation and participation was supported as a common cause, and a generosity of spirit was evident in public affairs. The more recent polarisation of political thought has, however, introduced social trends which are not so helpful. The radical right, with its emphasis on competitiveness and, in particular, its approach to raising educational standards, is creating a less caring attitude towards social and personal inadequacy. Consciences are apparently salved by charity rather than acceptance. The militant left has, on the other hand, become preoccupied by deviance in policy and behaviour. It is perhaps not without significance that special education comes under the heading of 'defectology' in Eastern Europe. While socially handicapping conditions are more clearly recognised, individual difference may be less tolerated. Somewhere in the middle ground, much harder to define and defend, is the recognition of the worth of all individuals which should be nurtured by society. This, coupled with the belief that government should create equal opportunities and limit the power of the successful to exploit the weak, is a necessary climate in which the special needs of individuals should be recognised.

The radical right tends to stress ability and achievement in relatively narrow academic terms, and separate grouping may be encouraged to limit what are seen as the contaminating effects of less motivated and less successful learners. The Assisted Places Scheme and the maintenance or reintroduction of selective schools are two examples of policies aimed to improve academic standards which may have adverse effects on children with special educational needs. The social purposes of education, the positive influences of comprehensive schools, and the personal and social developments of all young people may be subordinated in the interests of the academically able.

On the other hand, the radical left may tend to minimise individual differences and overstress the effects of adverse environments. Equality of opportunity may be equated with uniformity. Necessary special arrangements may not be made because of an unrealistic expectation of the ordinary school. Social objectives may take priority over educational ones.

Because the ordinary school programme is a major determinant of which children have special educational needs, social and political policies for the public education system have a major influence on special education. However, the effects of trends and changes in the political climate might be reduced if better informed public and political opinion recognised some of the common approaches to disability based on fundamental human rights. Public health services provide an interesting example which illustrates the point. In the last century many national and local political issues concerned community health and the supply of pure water. Now their provision is unquestioned by any shade of political opinion. Many of the efforts to enable those who are disabled to participate fully in all aspects of social life will similarly need to become generally accepted and non-political.

Social trends in special interests

The general consensus about the rightful place in society for those who are deemed to be handicapped is not yet easy to achieve. One stumbling block is the separate and hierarchical attitude fostered, albeit in some cases unintentionally, by different voluntary organisations and professional associations. There is still a pecking order of social concern and respectability reinforced by common public attitudes. Visual handicap gains most sympathy and moderate learning difficulties and maladjustment least. Organisations rival each other in gaining public attention, funds and special concessions. A coherent voice about common special needs is hard to detect. In England and Wales there is as yet no effective umbrella organisation representing the interests of all who are handicapped, nor is there a similar organisation effectively representing professionals working on their behalf. Sectional disability-orientated interests still dominate voluntary and professional efforts. A ministerial post with responsibilities for the disabled remains a token of intent while coordination is easily limited by departmental interests in government and a relative lack of cooperation between special interests. Similarly at local government level the different and often conflicting voices of many different groups are relatively easy to ignore. One of the major needs, now and in the future, is a more coherent approach to disability and the development of generally accepted policies which harness the efforts of the many associations and professional groups to achieve common goals.

An illustration of such an approach is afforded by the United States Special Education scene. Public law 94–142, passed in 1975, resulted from the sustained and coordinated efforts of many parents and disability organisations which together with the largest professional organisation, the Council for Exceptional Children, campaigned for legislation and lobbied Congress. After the law was passed various interests went their own way. However, when the Reagan administration proposed a review of legislation and the deregulation of special education, all the interests combined in a common cause to defeat the attempt. A united front and a well-argued case resulted in the confirmation of special education as an element in public education, which although liable to change, is unquestioned as a public service. More recently local disability alliances have been set up in many cities and towns in the United States representing all the sectional interests of those who are handicapped. These alliances present a unified approach to community needs which include combined fund raising, common stands on local issues and a coordinated approach to developing community provision and resources. Such an approach could be very effective in many communities in the United Kingdom.

An Agenda – Priorities for the Future

On the basis of existing experience, and taking account of the arguments in previous chapters, it is possible to outline an agenda for the future development of special education and suggest priorities for action. These are presented in sequence from birth to adult life, encompassing transitions between phases, and concluding with general considerations. Most of the suggestions are not new but they are often dealt with in isolation by those primarily concerned with phases and territories. By presenting them together as a kind of checklist it hoped that many more people working with children and young people considered handicapped will take a comprehensive view of special education and see their contribution in a broader context.

The early years

Even before birth it is important to recognise the adverse effects of drugs, smoking, alcohol and inappropriate diets on healthy foetal development. Ante-natal services can do much to reduce the incidence of disabilities. Appropriate genetic counselling may also enable prospective parents to know more about the risks of impairment and disability. Although the early detection of foetal abnormalities is now possible, the moral dilemma of terminating pregnancies remains unsolved. Much more certain is the evidence that effective gynaecological services and early paediatric intervention can reduce impairments and disabilities. A first priority is therefore to reduce the incidence of potentially handicapping conditions.

More severe physical and sensory disabilities and mental impairments will normally be detected at or soon after birth, and two aspects of services for parents and their children are critical. The first is counselling and support over a relatively long period. Many of the fundamental attitudes to disability are formed at this time as the anxiety and guilt of parents surfaces and as they need to mourn the loss of ideals. Counselling is necessary to enable parents to develop realistic attitudes and aspirations, to get to know the ways in which handicapping effects of disabilities may be reduced, and the services available to help them. The support of other parents with children with similar problems may be of considerable help. Thus health service personnel should be well informed about the personnel needs of parents at this time and about the social and educational services available to them. This is particularly important because parents place considerable weight on medical and nursing opinion at this stage.

Less severe disabilities and delays in development will emerge in the early years. These may be early indications of potential special educational needs. The primary health care team, of general practitioners and community nurses, has a crucial role to play in monitoring child development as has the social services team when problems may be discerned in adverse family circumstances, or where children show learning and adjustment difficulties in play groups, with child minders and in day nurseries.

The first important transition phase occurs in the early years when professionals in the health and social services may detect disabilities and significant difficulties in development and work with parents. Education provides services during this period including educational psychologists – who may work in child development teams (formerly district handicap teams) in the health service – peripatetic teachers – who may advise and work with parents in the pre-school years – and ordinary and special nursery schools and classes. Health and social services should know what the education service has available, and the education service should know which children may need special educational provision. Much more attention needs to be given to cooperative practices to ensure a smooth transfer of essential information between services and the introduction of parents to services other than those with whom they are first in contact.

A major priority is the future development of pre-school provision of all kinds. The value of appropriate early intervention is now unquestioned by professionals but not yet fully accepted as a priority by politicians and the public. As a result, such provision as is made to help young children with potential special education needs remains *ad hoc* and ill coordinated. What is required is a locally developed policy embracing the contribution of voluntary organisations, social services and education to produce a range of provision within which well planned intervention programmes can be made available. Such a strategy should be developed and maintained by a local multi-professional steering committee. For all children reliance on relatively unstructured play and on the general effects of natural growth and development is insufficient. The better the quality of adult mediation, the better the development of potential. For those children, therefore, whose early development is associated with disability and development difficulties sensitive and effective mediation is vital.

The school years

The second important transition point is entry to school at the age of five. Children whose special educational needs may be known will be helped to make a smooth transition if they are prepared for school and if the information their teachers need is passed on to schools by health, social and pre-school education services. However, less severe disabilities and learning difficulties may not be revealed before a child is exposed to the educational programme of a school. Thus the vigilance of teachers and the contributions of other professionals who work with them is vital if they are to be detected before their handicapping effects become more marked. Early school health examinations and early screening procedures are also very significant. The main point at this stage is not to earmark and label children as handicapped, with all the adverse effects which might accrue, but to start on a process of identifying potential special educational needs with a view to prevention where possible and to early intervention when necessary.

The ages from five to nine or ten in the primary phase are particularly important if a child is to remain a confident learner and develop a positive self image of himself in school. What is required is a range of special educational provision aimed at maintaining learning and social interaction within the primary school for as many children with learning difficulties as possible. Teachers on the staff with experience and preferably training in assessment, programme-planning and special teaching skills are the the first resource, together with materials and programmes to meet the more common difficulties. Where this is not possible, visiting advisory teachers should be available to help develop school-based solutions. In selected schools special classes and units should provide an integrated approach to more pronounced special educational needs, except where full assessment indicates the need to attend a special school or unit outside the school, full or part-time. The active development of special education in primary schools should have a high priority if at least some of the problems which arise in secondary schools are to be avoided.

The third significant transition point occurs at the time of transfer to secondary schools. The fact that transition is to take place may be an inhibiting factor. The staff of primary schools may not initiate the assessment of special educational needs because they believe a fresh start in the secondary school might minimise behaviour difficulties and provide renewed motivation to overcome learning difficulties. However, the process itself needs to be carefully planned for children with learning difficulties. Children with visual disabilities will need mobility practice in a new setting, those with hearing impairment will need to know where to seek visual information and children with physical disabilities may need to be confident about mobility around a new building and access to self care facilities. Other less successful learners may have orientation difficulties and problems in understanding new sets of of rules and procedures. Verbal preparation is not enough. Secondly, considerable attention is needed to the nature and quality of information about children's educational progress which is passed from school to school. Valuable time can be lost if a new school does not build on the previous experience of those who may be educationally handicapped. Records need to be more concerned with examples of children's work, the programmes they have followed and the skills and ideas they have mastered; they should be less concerned with relatively unsubstantiated gradings and teacher opinions of behaviour. There remains much to be done to establish what kinds of information are useful, how to record and how to transfer such information in an acceptable form.

During the secondary school period there should be three main priorities. The first is the active development of a school policy to meet both short- and long-term special educational needs, the second is a very close association between secondary schools and separate special schools and units, and the third is the active preparation for transition from school to adult life.

The school policy to meet special educational needs is, as has already been emphasised, closely linked with what is done in the regular programme to educate less successful learners. It involves senior management and heads of departments as well as special education teachers. Such a policy not only needs to deal with short-term needs for remediation but also with support throughout secondary education for other students with long-term learning difficulties and physical and sensory disabilities. It is no longer sufficient to add on extra help for those with limited literacy skills in the first three years. However, good models of secondary provision are not common, nor are they widely known, and much more effort is required to establish satisfactory patterns which can be adopted. Progress in the last forty years has been limited and other priorities, including examination success, have put the brake on developments: proper supporting arrangements for children with special educational needs in secondary schools are urgently required.

It is during this phase that extended curricular opportunities are available to young people, and individual personal and social development is particularly crucial to the development of the adult identity. For these reasons there should be a much closer association between separate special education and ordinary schools. On the one hand the curriculum of small special schools can be extended by close association with teachers in secondary schools and by individuals in special schools taking relevant courses in secondary schools. On the other, in a favourable atmosphere of care and concern for the individual, there are important opportunities for the youth age group to learn about each other and come to an acceptance of individual differences and disabilities. It is not easy to establish constructive and informed adult attitudes to disabilities and to minorities without shared experience and social interaction. Such an awareness is, however, necessary for those deemed handicapped if they are to develop realistic aspirations and relate to their contemporaries. The interaction between pupils following a secondary school programme, those receiving special education in the school and those receiving special education elsewhere needs to be actively fostered; not just in terms of their education experiences but more significantly for their personal development.

The final aspect of the secondary years which merits increased attention is the preparation for transition to adult and working life. This transition is currently made more difficult by the uncertain post-school situations. Not only are employment prospects uncertain but also opportunities for post-compulsory school education and training. The result is that both ordinary and special schools do not know for certain whether their preparation is to be complete because it will be the pupils' last contact with educational opportunities or whether it is to be the first phase of a process carrying on beyond school. Young people who are handicapped, and their parents, need information and sensitive counselling. The programme in their final school years should include personal and social skills, the development of self knowledge to make informed choices and an academic and vocational preparation for further education and training. Their teachers need a thorough knowledge of post-school options. They should be clear about the objectives of the final school years and they should work closely with other services. To help them in their work local authorities should develop a policy for transition, identify the range of possible options and keep schools well informed about them. All the effort put into special education in the earlier years may be dissipated unless its transitional phase is well planned.

Post-compulsory school

The options and ingredients of this phase have already been outlined. It is during this period that young people and their families can become confused about the responsibilities of different services and agencies. This will be due to some extent to the different criteria used to define handicap, and to some extent to the absence of a single point of reference to guide them through the map of possibilities. The period from sixteen to the early twenties is one where the effectiveness of earlier special education will be apparent and where a reasonable basis for adult life will be established. It is crucial that further education, vocational preparation, social skills training and the introduction into leisure activities is continued in a coordinated way if maximum autonomy, capacity to work and competence as a citizen is to be developed. The major needs of the young person with a disability or significant difficulty are clear, many of the techniques to meet them have been established, and many of the elements in a range of services both voluntary and statutory exist. What does not exist in many cases is a coherent and intelligible pattern of provision and support. This is in part due to different agencies planning in isolation. What is needed in each local authority area is a steering group, not dominated by one profession or department, but which identifies the range of needs and helps to plan an integrated pattern of courses, facilities and support services. Such a coordinating group should be sensitive to consumer interests, but also be able to balance the needs of the less articulate majority of young people with disabilities with those of the more successful, vociferous minority of similar young people.

The pattern of life which is now possible to envisage during the early adult years has three main requirements which, however severe the disability, should characterise provisions and services. The first of these is independent living. Just as many young people leave home to set up their own homes, so should those who are handicapped. Flats and houses in which small groups and married couples can live with the maximum independence and necessary support should be available. Continued training programmes may be necessary to develop essential skills in real situations. There are now many good examples of such arrangements, but they are not yet available to all who could benefit from them. Secondly, there is the right to work. At best this should be open, paid employment with an unprejudiced fair share of available opportunities. Failing this, community work, sheltered work and other forms of work including self care should be available which accord dignity, a sense of worth and reasonable remuneration. Finally, a range of social, leisure and recreational activities should be available, as far as possible in the same settings as for others in the community. If these are legitimate aims, then special education should be preparing for them with a balanced programme which covers all aspects of adult life.

General considerations

The agenda for the future of special education is formidable. The implications of new legislation and guidance are wide ranging and numerous. The context of social trends and ideas in which changes are taking place is confused and uncertain. Many consider that there are insufficient resources in manpower and money to make significant progress. More resources are needed but, before they can be claimed on a rational basis, it is necessary to consider what the main characteristics of a special education service should be in the future, how available resources should be allocated and what priorities should determine the pattern of future development. It is worth remembering that special education has always inched forward slowly, taking small steps and using limited resources, and has never been the subject of a major national financial investment programme except in buildings. There is no reason why future progress should be entirely dependent on new investment. Much can be done by changing practices.

Meeting special educational needs in ordinary schools has been discussed at some length in the previous sections. In summary, much will depend on the approaches developed to teaching the broader group of less successful learners found in most schools and on the appreciation that the majority of special educational needs and provision are relative to the effectiveness of the schools' work in this area. The major need is for development, evaluation and dissemination of patterns of provision which can become an integral and natural part of a school's work. These patterns will have to be acceptable to head teachers and others with management responsibilities. Only then will conditions be created in which special education teachers can plan an effective part in ordinary schools.

Whether or not ordinary schools become equipped to provide for a wider range of children with more complex and severe special educational needs, there will continue to be a need for centres where necessary teaching techniques for them, materials and equipment are developed and evaluated. Relatively isolated special units in ordinary schools do not provide the right conditions for these activities. Special schools are the obvious places for such centres. Some lines of development have been discussed in chapter 6. They will need to demonstrate outstanding qualities in curriculum development and programme planning, and will need to change from bases of care and protection to become fully integrated into a comprehensive education service with close links with ordinary schools. Some schools are moving in this direction successfully, but in order to function as a resource centre many more will need to prepare themselves by developing new skills and a more flexible response to changed circumstances. However, this process will not be easy unless local education authorities and regional special education conferences prepare a new map of provision within which they can set their contribution.

The introduction of new technology into special education will be a major task for the immediate future. It will be necessary to explore and define the new powers it can give to individuals with disabilities to communicate and to control their environment and learning material. At the same time, the objectives, content and methods of the curriculum will have to be reviewed to see how far new hardware can extend the range of learning opportunities. It will be a pity if new equipment is used, like the older teaching machines, solely for routine practice activities. If it is, motivation may be limited in the long run. There are now great opportunities to increase the range of experiences brought to those who are disabled and to present those experiences in ways which facilitate learning. In addition to mastering the use of new technology, there is a strong case for reconsidering the curriculum which can now be offered through it. To date the weakness has been that rather arid practice activities have been transferred to the new medium. The full exploitation of its potential is a major challenge for the future.

The way ahead for special education will not be easy unless its considerable strengths and its resources are reorganised within a conceptual framework which links it closely with the development of primary and secondary education, and which includes a rational approach to the post-school transition period. It is hoped that previous chapters in this book have demonstrated the existing range of provision and new elements and approaches which show promise. What also needs to be emphasised is the dedicated and strenuous efforts of a large number of special education teachers and other professionals who are devoted to helping children with special educational needs. However, many of these efforts are narrowly focused in isolated and separate situations, and many are managed by different administrators and advisers: a coherent approach to meeting special educational needs within local authorities and regions is not very evident. There has been more progress in assessing individual needs and planning programmes to meet them than in developing a rationale for special educational provision. The future of special education depends on tackling the task.

It is now possible to identify some principles which should determine a rationale, recognising that the practical planning of services will be influenced by local geographical, demographic and resource factors. Although there will be important national and regional elements in planning it is argued that an effective pattern of service delivery can only be developed by local authorities. In summary, it is suggested that the following principles should be accepted:

(i) *Planning special educational services is an integral part of planning the education service as a whole.* Because special educational needs are defined relative to the learning achievements of the majority, the organisations, curriculum and methods of ordinary schools, particularly as they impact on work with less successful learners, are major determinants of special educational needs. Thus, any major policy for ordinary schools should now include consideration of its special education aspects.

(ii) *Children with special educational needs should have the services they need provided within ordinary schools as far as is practically possible.* This implies greater attention to the process of integration and the continued development of cooperative and collaborative arrangements between special education teachers and their colleagues in ordinary schools.

(iii) *The purpose of provision outside ordinary schools should be clearly defined and the work of such special schools and units closely integrated with the work of ordinary schools.* Separate special education should not become a system of alternative provision. It should be seen as actively supporting the work of ordinary schools and providing a flexible system in which individual needs can be met, if possible in combination with ordinary schools.

(iv) *Pre-school special educational services are essential if the handicapping effects of disabilities and developmental delays are to be minimised.* Such provision should be seen as the essential basis for effective special education during the school period. There is a need for more active development of services not simply a minimal response to parental pressure.

(v) *Continued education and training beyond the age of sixteen up to the early twenties is essential if many of those deemed to be handicapped are to make an effective transition to adult and working life.* Minimising the handicapping effects of disabilities and significant learning difficulties requires a longer period of education and training. Increased personal competence, social adjustment, employability and decreased long-term dependence will only follow from a well coordinated post-school policy which is not solely dependent on parental and consumer demands.

(vi) *Administrative arrangements and responsibilities should en-*
      sure both the continuity of special education services from
      pre-school to post-school and their continuity with ordinary
      school provision for the less successful. This requires that at
      least one administrator has an overall view of the service
      to determine priorities and policies. It also requires that
      the work of advisers, psychologists and teachers with
      responsibilities for phases, for particular disability
      groups and for the quality of special education in ordin-
      ary and special schools is coordinated towards accepted
      objectives.

(vii) *Special educational arrangements should be developed on a*
       service-delivery model where the child needs them and not
       where the professionals prefer to work. The future develop-
       ment of a rationale for special education should recog-
       nise more clearly that the traditional institution as a base
       for special education is being replaced by a range of
       arrangements which require a more flexible response
       from professionals.

(viii) *The pattern of special educational arrangements should be*
        clearly stated in terms intelligible to ordinary teachers, parents
        and other professionals. Although this is a requirement of
        the 1980 Education Act there is still a long way to go in
        many areas before clear statements are possible particu-
        larly with respect to arrangements in and support ser-
        vices to ordinary schools.

Many may wish to amend or add to this list. It is presented for
two main reasons. First, many of those wishing to develop a
coherent system of special education have been frustrated in the
past by a lack of recognition that it is concerned with a large
percentage of the school population and, as such, is an essential
aspect of the work of ordinary schools. It is necessary to do away
with the false distinction between remedial education and special
education and continue to bring the administration and educational development of both within a common framework. The
traditional pattern of grouping special education separately with
school milk, transport and anything not directly concerned with
the primary and secondary school curriculum is changing, but
there is still much to be done to establish it as an essential strand
in planning the work of ordinary schools.

Secondly, unless these principles or a similar group are
accepted the efforts of many working in special education will be
less effective. Unless they receive clear leadership and can see

their work as part of a developing comprehensive service, they will continue to be frustrated. A strong lead must be given to ordinary schools in respect of meeting their obligation to less successful learners and those with special educational needs.

New arrangements and new patterns of service-delivery also require personnel trained to work in them. Traditional working practices, particularly those of many special education teachers, are changing rapidly. New skills are required and the training system has not yet responded sufficiently to these new demands. Nor, in its research functions, has it contributed sufficiently to a serious study of special education services and their future development. The rate of progress in future will depend on an informed and sensitive response by training institutions to new training needs. This response should embrace the training of all personnel, for example all teachers, as well as specialist personnel to work with those with special educational needs. Special education, important as it is, is nevertheless only one aspect of a community's response to and provision for its members who are handicapped in different ways and in different situations. It can do much to mitigate the handicapping effects of disabilities and significant difficulties but it can also unwittingly increase them if it presents the children and young people it serves as objects of charity. It must clearly demonstrate that it is helping to educate potentially contributing citizens capable of taking a useful part in the communities in which they live. This is the strongest message to emerge in recent decades: those considered handicapped are a minority with a contribution to make, not a dependent group to be cared for and absolved of responsibilities.

Envoi

This book has been an attempt to summarise the major issues confronting special education and the influences which may affect its development in the years ahead. It has been selective in its topics and drawn on experience both in the United Kingdom and elsewhere. More questions have been raised than answers given. But it is only by questioning and producing local solutions to problems that real progress can be made.

The material presented owes an inestimable debt to all those working in special education whose ideas have been shared generously over the years with the author. However, this is not to evade responsibility for their presentation. This is accepted in what has long been the tradition of counselling services. If the ideas are good they are the client's, in this case the reader's. If they are unacceptable, then of course they are the author's.

Bibliography

1 Special Educational Needs: The Warnock Report, HMSO, 1978
2 Hegarty, Pocklington & Lucas, *Educating Pupils with Special Educational Needs in the Ordinary School*, NFER-Nelson, 1981
3 'The Education of the Handicapped Adolescent – Integration in the School', OECD/CERI, 1981
4 Mary D. Wilson, 'The Curriculum in Special Schools', Schools Council, 1981
5 L. J. Gruenewald and J. Schroeder, 'Integration of Moderately and Severely Handicapped Children in the Public School System: Concepts and Progress', OECD/CERI: CERI/HA 79.07
6 'Educational Statistics in Schools', DES, 1982
7 E. Deno, 'Special Education as Development Capital Exceptional Children 37.3 229–237, 1970
8 Cope and Anderson, *Special Units in Ordinary Schools*, University of London Institute, 1977
9 B. R. Gearheart and M. W. Weishahn, *The Handicapped Child in the Regular Classroom*, The CV Mosby Co., St Louis, 1976
10 'Young Children with Special Educational Needs', DES, 1983
11 Norwegian seminar on integration, Dahlen Paper to OECD/CERI, 1982
12 Further Education Unit Publications:
     (a) *Experience Reflection Learning*, 1981
     (b) Developing Social and Life Skills, 1980
     (c) *Students with Special Needs in Further Education*, 1981
     (d) *Stretching the System*, 1982
13 Patricia Rowan, *What Sort of Life?*, NFER-Nelson, 1981
14 R. Gulliford, 'Integration and the Training of Teachers', OECD/CERI: Paper CERI/HA 84.02

Index